Crystals
for everyday living

Crystals

for everyday living

Brenda Rosen & Christina Rodenbeck

Bounty
BOOKS

Publisher: Samantha Warrington
Editorial & Design Manager: Emma Hill
Production Controller: Allison Gonsalves
Packaged by Guy Croton Publishing Services,
Tonbridge, Kent

First published in 2014 by Bounty Books,
a division of Octopus Publishing Group Ltd
Endeavour House,
189 Shaftesbury Avenue,
London WC2H 8JY
www.octopusbooks.co.uk

An Hachette UK Company
www.hachette.co.uk

Material previosuly published in *Crystal Basics*
(hamlyn, 2007) and *The Gaia Busy Person's Guide
to Crystals* (Gaia, 2006)

ISBN: 978-0-753728-50-5

A CIP catalogue record for this book is available
from the British Library

Printed and bound in China

CONTENTS

INTRODUCTION

Beautiful and mysterious, crystals have been used for thousands of years for decoration, adornment, protection and healing. Archaeologists have discovered beads, amulets, carvings and jewellery made of amber, jet, turquoise, lapis, garnet, carnelian, quartz and other crystals in excavations in every part of the world. Ancient people valued crystals for their magical and spiritual powers. Rulers wore rings and crowns set with precious gems. Shamans and healers used crystal amulets and gemstone remedies for healing and protection.

Crystals derive their power from the way they are created. The ancient belief that crystals are the bones of Mother Earth is not far from scientific truth. Millions of years ago, superheated gases and mineral solutions were forced upwards from the Earth's core towards the surface. As the molten rock gradually cooled, the mineral molecules formed orderly patterns.

The appearance of a crystal is affected by its mineral content, the temperature and pressure at which it formed and its rate of cooling. Hard and transparent crystals like diamonds were formed under tremendous heat and pressure. Softer stones such as calcite were created at lower temperatures.

Today we understand that the helpful properties of crystals arise from their structure. A crystal's molecules and atoms are arranged in a regular pattern that is repeated in exactly the same arrangement over and over in all directions. This orderly lattice-like structure gives crystals their unique ability to absorb, store, generate and transmit energy.

As you'll discover in this book, this ability allows crystals to be used to amplify, direct and balance the flow of life-force in your body and surroundings. You'll find that working with crystals is a gentle and natural way to improve your physical, emotional and spiritual wellbeing.

ENJOY THE WONDER OF CRYSTALS

You have opened this book, so you are entering a glorious Aladdin's Cave, where colours whisper secrets and crystals have amazing healing powers, where sparkle and glitter hide stores of wisdom.

Although crystal lore is old, perhaps as old as humankind itself, it has taken on many new layers in the modern era – which can be hard for both novice and expert to sort through.

It is an area that abounds with mumbo jumbo and hocus pocus. Together we can explore some of the myriad passageways, cul-de-sacs and odd ante-chambers of the crystal world, finding out what really works and what might just be a load of old rocks.

This user-friendly guide is your companion in the world of crystals, providing sensible advice and practical know-how. It is designed for the solo voyager, keen to explore on his or her own, although there may be occasions when you need to ask a partner to participate in some of the exercises. By the time you have finished reading it, you should have an excellent grounding in the principles of crystal work and feel confident enough to strike out on your own.

Working with crystals is particularly suited to the 21st century, since it can easily be slotted into a busy life. It helps if you can put aside a few minutes every day to at least touch your crystals, and perhaps spend a few moments focusing on them. But for the most part you will find your crystals ideal companions, silently working away for you as you get on with other things – nice to look at and responsive to your touch when the mood takes you.

HOW TO USE THIS BOOK

This book is designed to offer you a wide variety of practical ways to use crystals to improve your health, balance your emotions and access spiritual peace and harmony.

As with any guidebook, you are free to choose just how to use it to meet your needs. You can read it from cover to cover, starting at the beginning and going on to the end. This will give you the best foundation for further practice and study, as along the way you will learn all the basics of working with crystals from testing and caring for your crystals to particular healing techniques and layout to using crystals to stabilize the atmosphere of your home.

However, this book is also meant to be dipped into as a ready reference. It's a handy problem solver, meant to be used as an everyday manual for crystal work. Instead of having to plough through hundreds of words on each crystal, you can turn straight to a particular problem and implement the suggested cure. If you have a particular issue to be fixed, such as depression, a shortage of money or a lacklustre love life, you will find a crystal remedy within these pages.

If you do need a quick, pithy understanding of the properties of any of the most popular crystals available, then you should turn to the Crystal Directory on pages 168–173. When you go out crystal shopping, you may want to take this book with you.

This book will work in tandem with the crystals that you find, own and personalize. For example, your rose quartz may well turn out to be excellent for encouraging loving vibrations, but it may also be good for soothing headaches. Naturally, your personality and circumstances will affect the outcome of the work, but the more able you are to switch off and allow the crystals to work for you, the more effective will be your results.

INTRODUCING CRYSTALS

For as long as human beings have walked
this planet, we have been fascinated by
certain mysterious and beautiful stones.
Created in the dark heart of the earth,
crystals are a miracle of colour and light,
and so they have been treasured by people
of all cultures. Most crystals were made
by geological action over hundreds of
thousands of years. Before being mined,
some may have lain hidden in the earth
for millions of years – even since the very
formation of the planet. So when you hold
a crystal in the palm of your hand, you are
touching something beyond history, an
object that transcends time itself.

WHAT IS A CRYSTAL?

When chemical compounds or elements change from a liquid or vapour into a solid they usually take the form of crystals. In the process of solidification, the crystal develops geometrically, so the smallest particle has the same inner structure as the largest – salt and sugar are familiar examples of crystalline chemicals. In this book we will be focusing on crystals that are formed in this way and are used for healing, magic and personal development. They are those crystals that you generally find in shops labelled as crystals.

The atomic structure of crystals is what determines their shape. They can be made up of a single element – for example diamonds are pure carbon – or a combination. But the pattern in which the atoms join together, known as the lattice, is always consistent within a crystal type – this is how they are classified. For example, like diamonds, coal is pure carbon, but its lattice is completely different.

In the shop, crystals may look fairly similar in terms of shape. This is because many crystals are sold after they have been tumbled smooth, so you can't see their natural form with the naked eye.

Although crystals of the same family, say quartz, will always have the same inner structure, they may well come in a wide variety of colours – and even shapes. Some very valuable stones, such as rubies, are close first cousins to commoners such as hematite.

OPPOSITE: *An example of an hexagonal crystal formation, in this case Beryl.*

HOW DO CRYSTALS WORK?

Crystals are some of the simplest and most stable structures in the known universe – this may well be what gives them their power. They are made of repeated patterns of atoms or groups of atoms – molecules – connected together in a strong matrix.

Certain unique properties of crystals may explain why they work. First of all, all material is made up of a variety of different types of molecules that come together to create a single entity. For example, you are made up of an incredible variety of molecules that work together to create cells that create your unique self. Even, say, a pot of soil will contain many different types of minerals and vegetables that are jumbled together.

Secondly, many crystals – in particular quartz – contain a type of energy called piezoelectricity, which is due to floating positively charged sub-atomic particles trapped in the inner structure of the lattice. Piezoelectricity is released when the crystal is mechanically squeezed or subjected to an electric field – the crystal itself remains unaltered. Piezo electricity is a result of the crystal's very simple basic structure, which may also be the key to how these crystals help us.

RELEASING ENERGY FROM CRYSTALS

Sometimes only a very little bit of mechanical intervention can release this energy. Try rubbing a piece of amber and observe the static electricity you have made. This property is used in engineering, for example, quartz watches and radio transmitters. The piezoelectric charge generated using quartz is so precise that it is used to keep Greenwich Mean Time.

However, most crystals, by contrast, are simply one atom or molecule repeated ad infinitum. This means

A crystal cluster radiates positive energy and will inspire you with its natural brilliance.

Each sign of the zodiac has its associated crystals. These birthstones are traditionally associated with protection, luck and wisdom.

that on an electromagnetic level, each crystal gives off a single, consistent type of energy. Compare this with yourself – sometimes you're fast, sometimes you're slow, sometimes you're asleep, sometimes you're awake. Your mind, body, and spirit work in different rhythms and cycles – sometimes not always that consistently either. So, a crystal may work as a kind of sub-atomic metronome, giving your body a steady, dependable rhythm to lock into.

CRYSTAL HARDNESS AND SHAPE

Crystals are among the most symmetrical objects in creation, and tend to be symmetrical along all axes. This means there are actually only seven basic shapes that a crystal can take. These shapes are how geologists classify crystals, and they also give healers some ideas about how crystals can be used. Of course, there are always some exceptions to any rule and these are the amorphous crystals. Crystals can be classified in a number of ways, but the most useful qualities for practical purposes are a crystal's hardness, shape and colour.

2-3 Mohs: *Amber*

5-6 Mohs: *Lapis lazuli*

8 Mohs: *Emerald*

HARDNESS

In 1812, German mineralogist Friedrich Mohs (1773–1839) ranked ten commonly available minerals in terms of how easily they could be scratched. The Mohs scale is still the accepted standard of crystal hardness. As you might expect, the diamond scores a 10 on the Mohs scale, while talc, which easily breaks up into common talcum powder, scores a 1. Other crystals fall somewhere in between. Organic gemstones such as amber, coral and jet score 2.5–4. Lapis, opal and moonstone score between 5.5–6.5. Quartz, amethyst and gemstones such as emerald, sapphire and ruby score a 7 or above. Hardness is important when choosing crystals for healing and other practical purposes. Softer crystals can be used to absorb negative physical and emotional energy. It is the harder crystals that make the best choices for jewellery.

SHAPE

In their natural form, many crystals are rough, sharp or jagged – more like stones than translucent gems. Many of the small stones in crystal shops have been tumbled, a process that polishes a stone to enhance its colour and beauty. Polishing alters a crystal's appearance but does not affect its useful properties. A crystal's shape influences how it transmits energy.

Single-point crystals These focus energy in a straight line. In general, pointed crystals are used to transmit energy or draw it off, depending on which way the point is facing. A symmetrical crystal wand is likely to have been artificially shaped.

Double-terminated crystals These have a point on each end. Because they send and receive energy simultaneously, they are useful for balancing and integrating opposing forces, such as breaking up old patterns and overcoming addictions.

Crystal clusters These radiate their energy to the surrounding environment. They are useful for cleansing the energy in a room.

Geodes These have a cave-like interior that holds and amplifies energy, releasing it slowly to their surroundings. They are a good, relaxing choice for bedrooms.

Single point:
Citrine

Double terminated:
Clear quartz

Crystal cluster:
Amethyst

Geode:
Chalcedony

CRYSTALS AND COLOUR

Perhaps the most important quality for crystal healing is colour. As you may know, white light is really a mixture of colours, called a spectrum. A glass prism, a crystal drop hanging in a window or the raindrops in a sunny sky that create a rainbow all reveal that the seven colours of the light spectrum are red, orange, yellow, green, blue, indigo and violet.

Traditional Colour Meanings

Though you can certainly choose crystals for the colours that attract you most, here are some of the traditional meanings of crystal colours:

- **Red crystals** such as red jasper, carnelian and bloodstone increase your power, passion, courage and physical energy.

Carnelian

- **Orange crystals** such as carnelian, fire opal and orange calcite enhance self-esteem, confidence and creativity.

Orange calcite

- **Pink crystals** such as rose quartz, danburite and pink tourmaline foster kindness, love and compassion for yourself and others.

Rose quartz

- **Yellow crystals** such as citrine, amber and sunstone aid self-expression and encourage optimism and positive attitudes.

Citrine

You will already have experienced how colours affect your emotions. Wearing a bright red sweater can make you feel sexy, while sitting in a room with cool blue walls is soothing and relaxing. In colour therapy, a form of complementary healing that is becoming more widely accepted, the body is bathed in coloured light, or coloured crystals are placed directly on the body. Because of the links between the seven colours of the spectrum and your body's life-force (see pages 78–/9), a crystal's colour energy can be assimilated into your body's energy field through your optic nerve or, as some believe, directly through your skin, transmitting or absorbing energy as needed for a healthy balance.

- **Green crystals** such as green fluorite and green aventurine soothe the emotions and promote harmony and balance.

Green aventurine

- **Black crystals** such as smoky quartz, obsidian and labradorite are powerful protectors and help disperse negative energy and stress.

Obsidian

- **Blue crystals** such as blue lace agate, lapis and turquoise calm the mind, and cool and soothe the physical body.

Lapis lazuli

Clear quartz

- **White or clear crystals** such as clear quartz, apophyllite and moonstone promote new beginnings, peace and tranquillity.

- **Purple crystals** such as amethyst, lepidolite and angelite help develop intuition and spiritual knowledge.

Amethyst

HISTORY AND CRYSTALS

We live in an age of specialization. It's only in modern times that we have come to delineate a big difference between doctors, healers, magicians, scientists and astrologers. Previously, all these roles might well have been taken by one member of the tribe – the sage, wiseman or woman, shaman or seer. This person would likely have had some knowledge of the use of crystals in all his or her roles.

Crystals have been used in medicine, as amulets and as spiritual and psychic tools, since time immemorial. Jade has been found in prehistoric tombs, as well as black obsidian shaped into mirrors very similar to those used by modern scryers. Amber was also highly prized and routes were established across Europe to trade in it.

The royal blue stone lapis lazuli was clearly highly valued across Central Asia and the Indian sub-continent well before written history began. It has been found in tombs dating back 7,000 years in the Indus Valley. By 4500 bc, mining lapis lazuli had become an industrial process at Tell-i-Bakun in Persia.

It was not until the rise of civilizations in the Ancient Near East that we have written records of how humans used crystals. The Egyptians were fond of all kinds of crystals, especially blue ones such as turquoise mined in the Sinai Peninsula, and lapis lazuli, which was associated with the goddess Isis. Precious and semi-precious stones, or crystals, were used in the making of amulets to attract luck, ward off the evil eye, or bring fertility. Bloodstone was said to help to open locked doors.

Egyptian doctors at the time were also priests, and one of their jobs was to create amulets and spells for health. Surviving medical papyri explain how to use certain stones. For example, topaz, dedicated to the sun god Ra, was prescribed to relieve rheumatism. It seems that poultices and medicines were seen mainly as painkillers, while the cure itself was thought to be effected by magic.

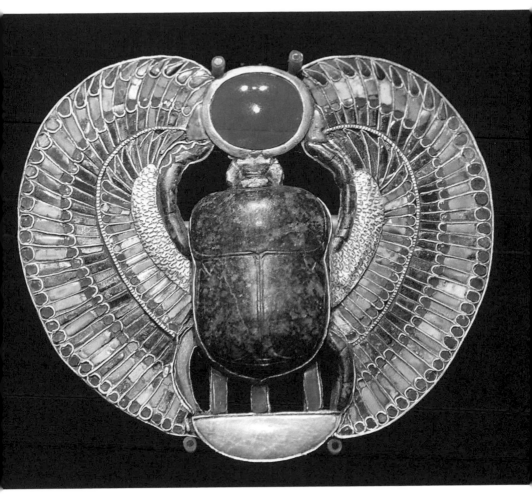

A pendant in the shape of a boat carrying a scarab, the symbol of the gods resurrection, flanked by two royal serpents. This is from the tomb of the Egyptian pharaoh, Tutankhamun.

A Jewish High Priest in his ceremonial clothes.

Bible Story

Crystals are often mentioned in the Bible, but usually only as a means of describing colour or great wealth. However, God gave precise instructions about the construction of the mysterious Breastplate of Judgement, which was to be worn by the high priest of Israel. No one knows what the precise significance of each stone was meant to be.

'And thou shalt make the breastplate of judgment with cunning work; after the work of the ephod thou shalt make it: of gold, of blue, and of purple, and of scarlet, and of fine twined linen, shalt thou make it.

Foursquare it shall be being doubled; a span shall be the length thereof, and a span shall be the breadth thereof.

And thou shalt set in it settings of stones, even four rows of stones: the first row shall be a sardius, a topaz, and a carbuncle: this shall be the first row.

And the second row shall be an emerald, a sapphire, and a diamond.

And the third row a ligure, an agate, and an amethyst.

And the fourth row a beryl, and an onyx, and a jasper: they shall be set in gold in their inclosings.

And the stones shall be with the names of the children of Israel, twelve, according to their names, like the engravings of a signet; every one with his name shall they be according to the twelve tribes.'

Exodus 28: 15–21

Meanwhile, the Chinese were already developing a passion for jade that was to last for millennia. Jade artefacts from the Songze culture (4500–3000 bc) can be seen today in the History Museum at Beijing. Jade was said to confer health, wealth and longevity. Even the search for jade was surrounded by taboos – only women were allowed to do it.

HISTORICAL PERSPECTIVE

The Indian tradition of gemology, which is still followed today, is extremely ancient. And like much Hindu lore, it has been written down and studied for many centuries – probably since about the first century ad. The art of studying and prescribing crystals was known as ratnapariska, as it is described in the Hame Sutra (c.700 bc). The most powerful amulet prescribed in ancient Hindu texts is the navaratna or nine-gem jewel. It is made up of a ruby, an emerald, a pearl, a coral, a jacinth, a tiger's eye, a topaz, a sapphire, and a diamond – each representing one of the seven planets and the north and south nodes of the moon.

In the Western tradition, the first written record we have of the medicinal use of crystals is in the treatise 'On Stones' by the Greek philosopher Theophrastus (372–286 bc), who was Aristotle's successor as head of the Peripatetic School in Athens. Theophrastus, a prolific classifier of the natural world, was the first to attempt to organize crystals into groups and describe them. He divided them into 'male' and 'female' crystals, which was later to cause some confusion, and he also assigned both medicinal and magical properties to some of them.

Theophrastus

A lapidary (mixed collection) of tourmaline crystals..

The knowledge of the Greeks was added to and embellished over the next 1,500 years or so in a series of books and treatises on crystals, or as they were more commonly called, precious and semi-precious stones, called lapidaries. These contain a mixture of geological, magical, and medical lore.

Possibly the most influential work was Pliny the Elder's *Natural History*. Written in the first century ad, it was to influence scholars and medical practitioners well into the next millennia. Pliny was a voracious collector of data, who liked to include a touch of gossip, opinion, innuendo and hearsay in most of his discussions of the natural world. This makes his *Natural History* entertaining, but somewhat dubious as a sourcebook.

Planetary amulets

The planets were believed to rule certain stones, plants and animals. These were combined to create magical talismans to fortify the wearer with the characteristics assigned to that planet.

- Sun – amber, chrysolite, topaz
- Moon – beryl, diamond, mother of pearl, opal, quartz
- Mercury – agate, carnelian, chalcedony, sardonyx
- Venus – emerald, jade
- Mars – bloodstone, hematite, jasper, ruby
- Jupiter – amethyst, aquamarine, blue diamond, sapphire, turquoise
- Saturn – jet, obsidian,onyx

ABOVE (FROM TOP LEFT, CLOCKWISE) *Smoky quartz, Red jasper, Onyx, Amber, Jade, Carnelian* (CENTRE) *Amethyst.*

In the 11th century the *Book of Stones*, written by Mabodus, Bishop of Rennes, was something of an international bestseller, since it was translated from Latin into eight other European languages. But it is Hildegard von Bingen (1098–1171) who probably most influenced modern crystal healers. Her book, *Physica*, details the natural history and curative properties of stones, herbs and animals. In it, she also recommends recipes and explains certain folk cures.

ELIXIRS AND POTIONS

Medieval lapidaries recommend either elixirs of particular crystals or the ground powder of certain others for medicinal purposes. One Pope was said to have swallowed a king's ransom in precious stones at a sitting.

Crystals were also assigned special meanings that would have been quite widely known at the time.

For example, Pope Innocent III sent King John of England four rings: the sapphire to represent hope; the emerald, faith; the garnet, charity; and the topaz, good works – none of which did him much good in the end.

The magical properties of precious stones were also thought to be enhanced by engraving. Precious stones – usually engraved with emblems, animals or astrological symbols – were widely prescribed as amulets. The tradition was thought to date back to Ancient Egypt, and some of the symbols used – such as the scarab on an emerald – were certainly of Near Eastern origin.

An ancient Egyptian brooch featuring a scarab carved in emerald.

Magical engravings

The Book of Wings, written in the 13th century by someone using the name Raziel, explains how each gem should be engraved to make its magic more powerful. Here is an extract:

'The figure of a falcon, if on a topaz, helps to acquire the good will of kings, princes, and magnates ...The well-formed image of a lion, if engraved on a garnet will protect and preserve honour and health, cures the wearer of all diseases, brings him honors and guards him from all perils in travelling.'

A passion for crystal

'I find it stated by medical men that the very best cautery for the human body is a ball of crystal acted upon by the rays of the sun. This substance, too, has been made the object of a mania; for, not many years ago, a mistress of a family, who was by no means very rich, gave one hundred and fifty thousand sesterces for a single basin made of crystal. Nero, on receiving tidings that all was lost, in the excess of his fury, dashed two cups of crystal to pieces; this being his last act of vengeance upon his fellow-creatures, preventing any one from ever drinking again from these vessels.'

Pliny the Elder

Pliny the Elder
(AD 23–79), *Natural History*

CRYSTALS TODAY

Since the rise of interest in alternative medicine, new spirituality and personal development in the 20th century, greater curiosity about the potential uses of crystals has developed. Some of this attention is based on the rediscovery of old lapidaries and magical treatises; much of this new regard is based on the re-evaluation of non-Western traditions, such as those of the Native American shaman and the Aboriginal 'clever fellows', and particularly Ayurvedic medicine as practised in India today.

It is important to remember, though, as you begin your exploration of the world of crystals, that a lot of the claims made for crystals are as yet unproved – and some are positively far-fetched.

Roughly, the uses of crystals can be broken down into three categories: physical healing or protection; emotional or mental support and healing; and spiritual and psychic growth and protection.

Decide what it is you want your crystals to do and be realistic in your expectations.

Clever fellows

Much of the oral tradition of the Aboriginal Australians is unavailable to outsiders. It is considered secret knowledge, passed on from father to son or mother to daughter, and kept within the tribe.

What data we do have is either considered unimportant by the Aboriginals themselves or is thanks to the work of anthropologists, who have been allowed to observe some of the shamanic rituals of Australia's 'clever fellows'. During these rituals, some of the men appeared to be pulling quartz crystals in great quantities out of their mouths. Whether or not this was sleight of hand, we don't know. What is certain is that the crystal is an important part of religious initiation.

When a child is born a sacred stone, called a churinga, is inscribed and placed in a cave, where it will protect and help the child for the rest of his life. Examples of churingas survive from the Stone Age.

One example of an Aboriginal healing crystal is mookaite, a kind of quartz oxide, that is good for regeneration, wound healing, and strength.

Churinga

PHYSICAL HEALING

Alternative medicine is often at its best when used to heal chronic conditions, such as arthritis – or certain conditions that conventional doctors simply find hard to diagnose. It also works well as an adjunct to orthodox treatments. For example, if you break a leg, you would probably like to have it set by a doctor and you might like to take some painkillers prescribed, but to enhance the healing process, you could wear malachite or meditate with calcite regularly.

Professional healers who use crystals usually have their own tried and tested battery of crystals – personalized by years of use. Reflexologists or masseuses may swear by a few well-used crystals – an amethyst or clear quartz, say – for helping to relax the muscles. Alternative midwives occasionally use healing stones in the labour room. These crystals are said to focus healing energy on the patient.

For your personal use, crystals should only ever be used as an extra, never as a substitute for qualified professional attention. Furthermore, you should always view your own efforts as an experiment: if you think a crystal is making you feel peculiar, then stop using it. Having said that, many practitioners report that the first three days of wearing or laying on of crystals may make you feel worse before you start feeling any benefit.

EMOTIONAL AND MENTAL HEALING AND SUPPORT

Crystals work well with the subtle energies of our moods and emotions. They can provide a steadying guidance when we are fighting our way through the emotional jungle and comfort if we fall into a depressive bog. If you are prone to mood swings, one of the grounding crystals, such as black tourmaline or tiger's eye, carried in your hip pocket may be all that you need to keep going.

Because of their consistent electric energy, crystals can facilitate clear thinking – very useful when writing books or studying for exams. Discordant atmospheres can be calmed using crystals; places where energy seems to have slowed down to a sluggish dribble can be jazzed up.

Crystals will help you clear your mind and prepare for difficult tasks ahead, such as exams.

Meditating while holding crystals in the palms of your hands is a powerful way of raising your spiritual and psychic awareness, whatever your personal circumstances.

SPIRITUAL AND PSYCHIC AWARENESS

The purity and simplicity of crystals can provide a straight and steady connection to the world of the spirit – no matter what your belief system. They can also enhance our awareness of the infinite mystery that is life in a positive way – and help us to connect appropriately to that mystery.

The best way to start exploring a crystal's numinous connection is to spend time meditating with it. The vibration between you and the crystal is unique but repeatable, so that if you find that you respond very well to a particular crystal the first time, it should become easier and more effective the more you use it.

In general, violet, white or transparent crystals are connected with the spiritual plane. Try using angelite, amethyst or clear quartz to begin with.

Amulets

It's true to say that in most of the world today jewellery still has a sacred or amuletic purpose that is deemed more important than its decorative use. The most widely used amuletic crystal is turquoise, which is treasured by Native Americans, Tibetans and other tribes of Central Asia. Because of its colour, turquoise is associated

Red crystals have long been favoured for use in amuletic jewellery.

with the sky, rain and water. It also has a tendency to change colour with age, which makes it almost seem like a living creature.

The red carnelian also has a long tradition of use as an amulet, particularly in Central Asia, where it is the most popular magical crystal – it is associated with blood and the worship of fire, passion and the universal life energy that permeates all things.

Jade is still popular in China today, where its magical ability to attract prosperity and health is valued as much as its beauty. The simple jade pi – a disc with a hole through the centre – is worn as a protective amulet all over the Far East.

MEDITATING WITH CRYSTALS

Crystals are a great tool for keeping the mind focused during meditation. You can either touch or simply look at a crystal when you are meditating. What is important is to allow yourself to enter the right state of mind first. A good crystal to start with is clear quartz, but as you become more experienced, you will want to choose crystals to meditate with that have the energy that suits your needs or mood of the moment.

• Find a quiet place where you will not be disturbed. Make sure your clothing is loose and comfortable, and that you will not be too hot or too cold if you sit still for half an hour or so.

• Choose one crystal. If you intend to look at it, place it close so that you can easily see it without having to move. If you are holding it, keep it in your left hand.

• Once you have picked your spot, get into a comfortable position. If you can sit cross-legged without pain for a long period, then try that. Most people, though, will find that sitting in an upright chair is perfectly good.

• If you are sitting, make sure that your spine is straight, but not like a ramrod. You should feel as if your head is floating on top of your spine; everything should feel loose and flexible. This is important for your breathing: the key to meditation.

• Take a few deep breaths in through your nose. Let your breath fill your lungs. Imagine that you are expanding your lungs to the back as well as the front. Let the air out slowly.

• Now consciously relax your body, starting with your toes and working up. You can do this quite quickly, imagining that you are letting go of tension with each exhalation.

• Now that you are completely relaxed, notice your breath gently sliding in and out of your nostrils. It should be quite delicate.

• Focus on your crystal. Allow its colour to enfold you. Feel its energy around you. Lose yourself in the crystal. If you are just gazing, allow your eyes to go out of focus. Every time your thoughts begin to drift, return to the crystal.

• If you are holding your crystal, allow its energy and colour to spread up your arm, into your body and fill the air around you. Again, every time your mind begins to drift, return to the crystal energy.

Hold the crystal in your left hand as you gaze at it and lose yourself in your thoughts.

WORKING WITH CRYSTAL ENERGY

If you are just beginning to work with crystals, this chapter provides basic information about choosing, cleansing and energizing your crystals. If you do not own any crystals, to get started you'll need a piece of quartz with a natural point and a few round or oval crystals about the size of a walnut. A good initial purchase might include a clear quartz point and small tumbled pieces of amethyst, blue lace agate, rose quartz, tiger's eye and red jasper. If you already have a collection of personal crystals, you'll find helpful tips in this chapter about preparing your crystals for practical use.

BEGINNING WITH OPTIMISM

Why not start your collection with a single crystal that brings you joy? Make this a 'wake up and smell the coffee' crystal; a crystal that you want to look at first thing in the morning; a crystal that makes you leap out of bed feeling energetic, lively and focused.

The first crystal you choose is crucial. It will set the tone for the whole enterprise – creating a special energy in your home that will work with each new one you acquire.

Wake up and smell the coffee crystals

Crystal	Effects
Beryl (yellow, golden)	Dynamism, clear-sightedness, optimism
Citrine	Self-confidence, individuality, mental stimulation
Emerald	Harmony, truthfulness, trust
Fire opal	Success, sexual energy, inner fire, high spirits
Garnet (red, pink, or orange)	Courage, joy, grabbing the future
Ruby	Fire, pure energy, joy
Green tourmaline (verdelite)	A sense of wonder, joy

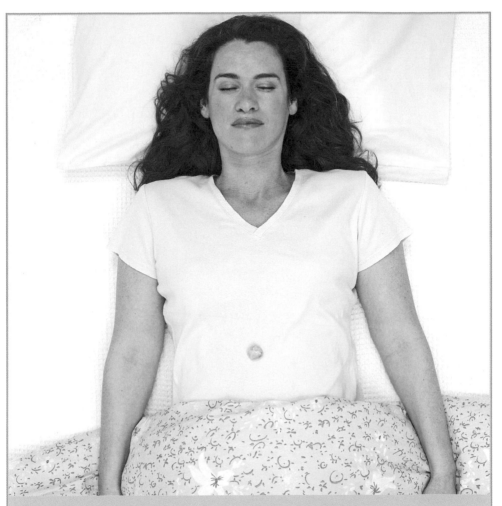

The crystal used in this picture is citrine.

Morning meditation

Keep your crystal beside your bed. As soon as you wake up, take it and put it on your solar plexus (see pages 82–83). Close your eyes and focus your mind on the healing energy emanating from the stone through your body. Imagine the colour of your crystal as a warm glow that spreads through your body from the top of your head to the tips of your toes. Now imagine it filling the air around you – float there for a while. When you are ready, open your eyes and start your day.

CHOOSING YOUR CRYSTALS

Putting together a crystal toolkit should be fun – and not too expensive. First of all, you should take a look at any crystals that you may already own. That means looking at all your jewellery. Some practitioners say that a crystal with a hole doesn't work, but this does not seem to hold true. You may be surprised to find out just how many crystals you have floating around your home. Try to identify your crystals. If you cannot, take them to a jeweller who will do it for you.

Now check to see if any of the crystals you already own are useful to you. You may be surprised to find that you are already wearing one – a diamond perhaps – that does serve a need. The crystals you already own are powerful because they are imbued with your energy.

Next you will need to acquire some clear quartz. This is the most versatile and useful of all rocks, so you should get quartz in various

You should feel comfortable with all your crystals. Does it feel good in the palm of your hand?

Single- and double-terminated crystals

Also known as points, single-terminated crystals are used to direct energy. In order to draw negative energy away from the body, aim the points outwards. To draw positive energy in, point them towards the subject. Double-terminated crystals have two definite points so the energy is channelled, radiated or absorbed in two directions simultaneously.

Clear quartz

shapes. Don't bother pursuing rarer examples, but a set of, say, four single-terminated clear quartz crystals (points) will come in handy time and time again. In fact, you may find that this is all you need as

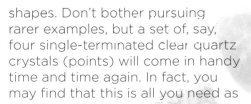

the 'points' will effectively channel energy towards the tips. You will be able to use them for all kinds of mental, emotional, and even physical healing; for cleansing other crystals and even for Feng Shui.

Dos and don'ts when crystal shopping

Do

- Take your time.
- Use your intuition.
- Enjoy yourself.
- Touch the crystals.
- Get sidetracked.
- Be prepared to give away crystals that don't work for you.

Don't

- Be seduced by big, glittery crystals.
- Feel that the more you pay, the better the crystals.
- Go mad with your cheque-book and buy the shop.
- Forget that you can always come back another time.

FORMS AND VARIATIONS

Crystals come in all shapes and sizes – from great rough rocks to delicately worked jewellery.

Rough or raw crystals

Crystals in their natural state (left) often have very powerful vibrations that can change the atmosphere of a whole room. The energy tends to be gentle, natural and diffused.

Points or wands

Also known as single- and double-terminated crystals (left). Check to see if the point is naturally occurring or whether it has been worked – some practitioners believe that natural points are more effective. This type of crystal is an energy transmitter and excellent for healing.

Onyx

Single-terminated clear quartz

(Left to right) *Clear, rose, smoky quartz*

Clusters and geodes

These crystals (right) also produce high energy. Large clusters or geodes (hollows filled with crystal) are powerful energy generators and can sometimes have an overwhelming effect in a small space.

Tumbled stones

These have been polished in a machine (see below). The effect is that the energy radiates more evenly, so they are excellent for laying on the body or carrying in your pocket.

Slices

These often reveal the inner beauty of a crystal structure (right). In traditional crystal healing, if the shape thus revealed corresponds with a particular part of the body, it is specially powerful.

Amethyst

Agate, dyed mauve

SET OF STARTER CRYSTALS

Start with a few crystals and gradually expand your collection – you shouldn't feel in any hurry. The selection here is a good start, because these crystals will address the most common problems you come across. They are easy to get hold of and, as a rule, are reasonably priced and versatile. But do not feel bound to start with them. If you are unaccountably drawn to some other crystals, choose those. However, the idea is to achieve a fairly balanced selection of crystals rather than having a whole bunch that only offer a similar set of solutions.

Blue lace agate

Basic Crystal Set
Agate (blue, grey, green, and brown)
• Good luck and protection
• Growth, stability, and maturity

Blue lace agate
• Feminine energy
• Harmony

Moss agate
• Green fingers
• Making new friends

Amethyst (violet)
• Harmony, enlightenment, and connection to spirit
• Wisdom and tolerance
• Good for meditation

Carnelian – also known as sard (red, orange, yellow, and brown)
• Courage and action
• Ability to finish projects
• Physical energy

Citrine (yellow)
• Confidence; anti-depressant
• Mental clarity, dynamism, and initiative
• Good digestion

Clear quartz
• Focusing energy of all kinds
• As a stand-in for any other crystal
• Simple tumbled clear quartz is fine, but try to get hold of some quartz points as they will prove invaluable

Lapis lazuli (dark blue)
- Wisdom, kindness, and love
- Protection from negative energy in all environments
- Peace and harmony

Malachite (dark green)
- Prosperity, money luck, and sensual appreciation
- Healing past hurt
- For stimulating healing dreams and revealing subconscious yearning

Obsidian (black)
- Insight
- Grounding and protection from negative influences
- Dissolving pain

Peridot (green)
- Mental, emotional, and physical detox
- Healing
- Used in the Middle Ages to ward off evil spirits

Red jasper
- Courage
- Grounding
- Physical strength and sexual energy
- Honesty
- Speed energy up
- Yellow jasper has a calmer energy and green jasper has a more balanced energy

Rose quartz (pink)
- Love
- Self-healing and love

Smoky quartz (pale grey to dark brown)
- Grounding and protection against bad luck
- Dissolving pain

Sodalite
- Wisdom and insight
- Listening and speaking skills
- Organisation
- Counters harmful radiation

Tiger's eye
- Protection and grounding
- Trust and common sense
- Slows energy down
- Good for starting new ventures with both feet on the ground

Turquoise
- Protection – particularly from ill-wishers and on long journeys
- Connection to spirit
- Mentally and spiritually uplifting
- One of the most widely used crystals for amulets

Turquoise

GROUNDING

Grounding is a term that is regularly used these days. Essentially, it means keeping a grip on reality by maintaining your connection to the earth. If you ever engage in any spiritual work or healing, it's important to make sure you are grounded when you finish – try stamping your feet or drinking a glass of water. When you are working with crystals, always use a grounding crystal as part of your set.

Many of us – especially sensitive types – find it quite difficult to stay grounded in the everyday. We have a tendency to daydream or let our mind drift off when we should be concentrating on matters at hand. This is exacerbated by the unnatural pace of modern life. Simply carrying one of the grounding crystals in your pocket can work wonders.

When grounding can help

You may need to work on grounding if:

• Your relationships don't last.

The crystals used in this picture are hematite.

- Your career is just a job.

- You can't make your mind up and have trouble focusing on the project in hand.

- You jump from fad to fad.

- You daydream a lot.

- You often feel sort of 'floaty'.

- You feel you are a drifter.

- You attract emotional leeches.

Grounding exercise

Allow yourself some time with this exercise initially. But as you get the hang of it, it should only take you a minute or two to feel grounded. You may literally feel a pleasant kind of downward-pulling energy.

- Sit somewhere comfortable where you will not be disturbed.

- Hold a grounding crystal in each hand, and rest them gently on your thighs.

- Close your eyes and focus on your breathing. Watch the air flowing gently in and out of your nostrils.

- With each exhalation, imagine that thoughts and ideas are emptying from your mind. With each inhalation, imagine a clear light sweeping through your body and bringing in clean, new energy.

- When you are feeling refreshed, feel the energy of the crystals in your two hands. Feel it flowing up your arms and filling your torso. Feel it flowing down your

body and through your spine into the floor. Feel it flowing through each leg and down through the soles of your feet. Imagine this energy rooting into the earth, connecting you right down into the soil like a tree. If you are good at visualizing, imagine yourself growing these roots.

- You are now fully grounded. When you are ready, open your eyes and carry on with your crystal work.

Red jasper

TESTING YOUR CRYSTALS

You can test your reaction to specific crystals using a technique called kinesiology. You may have come across kinesiology in relation to food allergies. It requires a partner to work with, but it's by far the clearest way of checking your reaction to the many different crystals available.

This system is sometimes called muscle-testing, because it relies on checking the strength or weakness of your right arm muscles. A crystal that agrees with you will strengthen your muscles or have no effect, while one that saps your energy will weaken them.

The Test
(01) Standing up straight, but comfortably, stretch your right arm from the shoulder horizontally. Hold it out in front of you so that it is flexible and can be moved around, but not floppy.

(02) Using her right palm, your partner should push gently down on your arm and see how much resistance she meets as she does this. This will give her an idea of what your natural resistance is to being pushed.

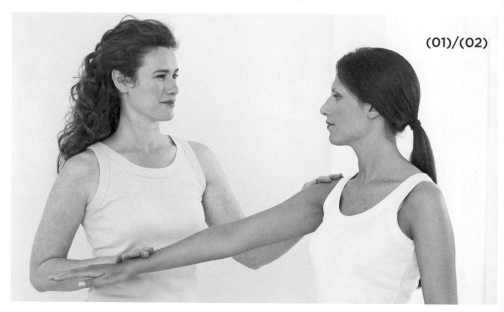

(01)/(02)

(03) Hold the crystal to be tested in your left hand at waist height. Give it a little time to warm up.

(04) When you are ready, hold your right arm out again, and let your partner push gently down in the same way as before. If she meets more resistance than before, take this as a 'yes' the crystal agrees with you. Your arm may even bounce up a little when she lets go. If your arm seems to have become more relaxed, that's a 'no'.

CARING FOR YOUR CRYSTALS

The crystals you have are a precious gift and it's up to you to look after them and keep them in top condition. This means keeping them in a sensible place, adjusting their programming when necessary and cleansing them.

LOOKING AFTER YOUR CRYSTALS

Once you have chosen your crystals, look after them carefully. Crystals are like wise and treasured friends, so treat them with respect. Softer crystals and crystals with unusual shapes, such as points and clusters, can be fragile. To keep them safe, wrap each one separately in a silk scarf. Alternately, find the right place in your home or office for each crystal, such as on your desk, on your bedside table or as part of an arrangement of houseplants near your favourite chair.

Though harder natural stones can scratch softer ones when they are stored together in a pouch, tumbled stones are in general more resistant to damage. It's perfectly fine to keep a collection of small tumbled stones in a silk bag or pouch.

Tumbled crystals can be stored in a silk pouch.

Examine your crystals from all angles, paying close attention to the feelings that they arouse.

The assorted crystals in this bowl are all in need of a thorough cleansing. This can be done in a variety of ways, using water, sage smoke, rock or sea salt or even sunlight – the choice is yours (see these pages and overleaf). Some people add essence of rosemary to the water they use for cleaning crystals, as this is widely believed to draw out negative energy.

A beautifully clean clear quartz single point crystal.

CLEANSING A CRYSTAL

When crystal healers talk of cleansing a stone, they mean more than getting rid of any dirt. What you are doing is clearing the energy of the crystal and helping its unique vibration to resonate effectively.

When you first acquire a crystal you should cleanse it thoroughly. This is especially true if you bought it from a shop or if it was previously used by someone else. A good wash in soapy water should be your first step, if only to get rid of any accumulated grease and grime. The exception is if you found the crystals yourself in its true environment – on a river bed or in the earth, for example. If the latter is the case, you may want to retain the vibes of its place of origin. If you are able to return to the crystal's place of origin once in a while, you may want to take it along with you for a little refreshment.

RUNNING WATER

Holding a crystal under a tap is often enough to refresh the crystal. Put it under cold running water – either keep the crystal in your hand or put it in a glass receptacle and let the water wash over it. Alternatively, bathe it in water mixed with salt or immerse it in a natural water source such as a stream, waterfall or the sea. As the water flows over your crystal, hold the intention that all negative energy is being washed away and the crystal is being re-energized. Halite and selenite are actually water-soluble, so this solution won't do.

You should wash your crystals (right) or use the smoke from a sage smudge stick (above and overleaf) to clean them thoroughly.

Hematite being cleaned in rock salt.

Rhodonite being cleaned in salt water.

ROCK OR SEA SALT

Salt can be quite harmful to some crystals – for example opal is ruined by contact with salt; however, it is a highly effective cleansing agent. To use the salt energy without affecting the crystal, put the crystal in a glass dish and then embed the dish in the salt. Leave it for a day or more.

SEA OR SALT WATER

Clean sea water is a wonderful cleanser – especially if you have a crystal that you feel is very damaged. If you can't get hold of any sea water, try mineral water mixed with sea salt. Be generous with the salt, and leave the crystal in the salt water overnight. Some practitioners swear by putting the container in the light of the full Moon.

SUNLIGHT

Leaving the crystal in the full light of the sun will also energize the stone. It is an especially useful method for those crystals that already have a sunny energy, such as citrine, ruby or sunstone. Amethyst, rose quartz and turquoise sometimes fade in sunlight, so this method is not suitable for them.

SMOKE

Native Americans traditionally cleansed their crystals with white sage or sagebrush smoke. Sage for

Smoking sagebush and sodalite.

Sunstone enjoying full sunlight.

'smudging' is fairly easy to get hold of in shops. Simply light the sage and either allow the crystal to sit in the smoke or pass it through the smoke. All crystals can be cleansed by being surrounded by the smoke from a sage smudge stick. This method is especially useful for large crystals or for cleansing several crystals at once.

MOONLIGHT

All crystals can also be cleansed by bathing them in the light of the moon for a few hours. Place a crystal on your windowsill or in your garden and allow the moonlight to draw off any impurities in order to recharge the crystal's energy.

Moonlight is an effective crystal cleanser.

ENERGIZING YOUR CRYSTALS

After you have cleansed a crystal for the first time, you can energize it for its particular task. Hold it in your hands and concentrate on the purpose for which you wish to use it. For instance, say to yourself or out loud, 'I dedicate this crystal to healing' or 'I dedicate this crystal to bringing more love into my life.'

If you are not sure how you will use a crystal, you can dedicate it to a general positive purpose such as 'the highest good for all'. You may wish to repeat this process several times with a new crystal.

BIG ROCK

Leaving a crystal in the nest of a crystal cluster can help readjust its vibrations, but be sure the cluster is itself OK. Amethyst and quartz

Amethyst cluster with raspberry garnet.

Try clear sound vibrations as a way of energizing your crystals.

clusters are especially favoured for this method of cleansing. A set of single-terminated clear quartz crystals pointing inward in a circle around the crystal to be cleansed also works.

SOUND

Clear sound vibrations are an excellent way of tuning a crystal – a singing bowl will clear a group of crystals in minutes. Simply put the crystals in the bowl then tap it and allow the note to resonate through the stones. You can do the same with a tuning fork by holding it next to a single crystal. Theoretically, anyone with a good singing voice should be able to purify a crystal by maintaining a single pure note. This could also be a good way of truly personalizing your collection.

TUNING AND PROGRAMMING YOUR CRYSTALS

Each of your crystals is sending out a subtle electro-magnetic vibration; each is doing its own thing. Because the lattice of each crystal is such a simple structure, the vibrations of a crystal are especially pure and consistent – which may be what gives them their special and unique healing properties. You should remember this when you start to programme your crystals.

CHOOSE THE RIGHT CRYSTAL

First of all, be sure that the purpose you have chosen for the particular crystal is an appropriate one: a fire opal is unlikely to be much good at calming a situation down for instance; and all the will-power in the world won't force an agate to become a warrior.

BE CLEAR IN YOUR PURPOSE

Next, think about the exact purpose you have in mind for this crystal – the clearer your intention, the more effective the programming. Try to think up a precise phrase that sums up what you want to do with this crystal. For example, 'I want to enhance family harmony', or 'I want this crystal to promote open communications'.

Then, take the crystal in your left hand and feel it warm against your skin. See if you can sense the single-note vibration coming from the stone. Think about how it feels. Check to see if your intended purpose for the crystal fits the crystal.

SAYING YOUR PHRASE

Next, say your phrase out loud, as the voice is always more effective than the mind alone. But if you are shy about it, simply repeat the phrase in your mind.

You may have to repeat this process several times before it begins to work, but you will find that the more you use the phrase for its special purpose, the more effective it becomes.

The art of using crystals effectively lies in ensuring they are correctly programmed and tuned to your precise personal needs and purposes.

Once you have energized and tuned your crystals, energize yourself by wearing them as jewellery.

CRYSTAL PLACEMENT AND ESSENCES

These guidelines about placing, wearing and carrying crystals and using gem essences will help you to get the most benefit from the crystal exercises in this book.

PLACEMENT ON YOUR BODY

Many of the crystal exercises involve placing crystals on your chakra points or around your body. You'll find these most helpful when you are relaxed and uninterrupted, so close the door to your room, turn off your mobile phone and give yourself permission to focus solely on yourself. Prepare a place where you will be comfortable lying on the floor, on a yoga mat or a folded blanket.

PLACEMENT IN YOUR SURROUNDINGS

Larger crystals are a natural way to bring balance and beauty into your home or office. Place crystals in any room where you spend time, such as the bedroom, office or lounge. Be sure to keep these display crystals clean by dusting them regularly using a soft cloth or feather duster.

WEARING AND CARRYING CRYSTALS

Crystal jewellery, such as pendants, rings or earrings, infuses you with continuous energy throughout your day. Also try carrying a crystal you are working with in a small silk pouch in your pocket or bag.

GEM ESSENCES

Gem essences have a subtle and gentle healing effect. They can be rubbed on an affected part of your body, poured into your bathwater or put into an atomizer bottle and sprayed around a room.

Crystals of any kind placed carefully around your home will give it life and energy.

There is so much beautiful jewellery made from crystals to choose from.

Wearing crystal jewellery of any kind will bring balance and harmony to your life.

How to Prepare a Simple Gem Essence

1 Place a cleansed crystal that can be immersed in water in a clean glass bowl filled with spring water. (If the crystal should not be immersed in water, place it in a small glass bowl and place the small bowl in a larger water-filled bowl.)

2 Place the bowl where it can stand in the sunlight for several hours.

3 Remove the crystal and pour the essence into a glass bottle with an airtight stopper. To keep an essence for more than a week, double the volume of the liquid in the bottle by adding clear alcohol or vodka as a preservative.

4 Label your essences with the crystal's name and the date of preparation. Store them in a cool, dark place.

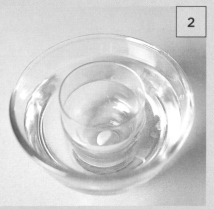

UNDERSTANDING CRYSTAL HEALING

Healing yourself is a uniquely personal process. The first step is awareness. You train yourself to listen to the messages your body is sending and use your intuition to figure out what your body needs. Sometimes, although what you are experiencing is a physical symptom like a headache or a digestive upset, the underlying cause is a combination of physical, emotional and even spiritual factors. Working with crystals gives you the opportunity to tune into what's happening at all of these levels and to stimulate your body's natural ability to heal.

CRYSTALS AND YOUR BODY

Though healing with crystals feels very modern, the practice is actually very old. The earliest records of crystal healing come from ancient Egypt. The Ebers Papyrus (1550 BCE) gives remedies for many illnesses and lists the medicinal uses of various gems. Healing with crystals is also mentioned in India's Ayurvedic records and in traditional Chinese medicine from around 5,000 years ago. Native American shamans used sand coloured with ground gemstones in their healing rituals.

ENERGY

The theory behind crystal healing is simple. In addition to its physical parts, your body has an energy system. Traditional healing methods focus on regulating the flow of energy through the chakras and channels that link every part of your anatomy. You can readily experience the effects of this energy flow. On days of high energy, you find it easy to get things done, but when your energy is blocked, you may feel tired or confused.

When you are ill, some aspect of your body's energy is out of balance. Illness may be your body calling your attention to a life issue you have ignored for too long. Focusing your awareness on your condition encourages you to make better lifestyle choices and address both your symptoms and their underlying causes.

THE EFFECT OF CRYSTALS

Crystals are superb energy transmitters. Their crystalline

Amethyst is an excellent example of a crystal with good, all-round healing properties.

Blue stones such as agate and chalcedony are good for healing conditions of the upper chakras.

structure amplifies your healing intentions and restores and rebalances your body's energy by removing blockages, drawing off excess energy and shoring up weaknesses. Crystal healing is not a substitute for traditional medical care, but it can help in many practical ways. Healing with crystals also empowers you to take personal responsibility for your health, using simple, natural methods that you can believe in.

The crystal healing chart on pages 70–71 shows that the link between a specific crystal and a health problem is often based on the crystal's colour and frequency of vibration or subtle electromagnetic field. Crystals with a lower vibration (red, orange and yellow crystals) heal conditions related to the lower chakras, while crystals with a higher vibration (green, blue, indigo and violet crystals) work best on conditions of the upper chakras.

USING THE CRYSTAL HEALING CHART

You'll find instructions throughout this chapter for using healing crystals, but this chart can help you to choose the right crystal quickly and easily. To use crystal energy to support or

CHAKRA	RELATED BODY PARTS	POTENTIAL HEALTH PROBLEMS
ROOT	pelvis, bones, legs, ankles and feet, hips and rectum, immune system	sciatica, varicose veins, pelvic pain, rectal tumours, haemorrhoids, problems with hips, knees, ankles and feet
SACRAL	sexual organs, large intestine, kidney, bladder, appendix, lower spine	lower back pain, premenstrual tension, infertility, impotence, bladder infections, appendicitis, kidney stones
SOLAR PLEXUS	stomach, liver, spleen, gallbladder, pancreas, small intestine, middle spine	ulcers, colon cancer, diabetes, indigestion, eating disorders, hepatitis, gallstones, constipation, diarrhoea
HEART	heart and circulatory system, ribs, chest, lungs, shoulders and arms, breasts, upper spine	high blood pressure, heart disease, bronchitis, asthma, pneumonia, shoulder problems, breast cancer
THROAT	throat, neck, mouth, teeth, gums, jaw, thyroid, neck vertebrae, oesophagus	sore throat, laryngitis, frequent colds, gum disease, dental problems, thyroid problems, swollen glands, stiff neck
BROW	brain, central nervous system, eyes, ears, nose, sinuses, pituitary gland, pineal gland	epilepsy, eye problems, sinus infections, headaches, migraine, stroke, deafness, insomnia, nightmares
CROWN	whole body systems: skeletal system, muscular system, skin, neurological system	chronic exhaustion without physical cause, skin diseases, environmental illness, neurosis, mental illness

relieve a physical, emotional or spiritual condition related to a particular chakra, place one of the listed crystals on the chakra and leave it in place for 20 minutes while you relax quietly.

CRYSTAL COLOURS	HELPFUL CRYSTALS
red, dark red, greenish-red, brownish-red, red-black	smoky quartz, garnet, bloodstone, ruby, red jasper, red beryl, red calcite, red agate
orange, reddish-orange, yellow-orange, orangey-brown, peach	carnelian, orange calcite, citrine, tangerine quartz, fire opal, orange aragonite, moonstone
golden yellow, lemon yellow, honey-coloured, gold	amber, yellow jasper, yellow tourmaline, golden topaz, tiger's eye, citrine, rutilated quartz, yellow calcite, sunstone
pale pink, bright pink, rose pink, pale green, emerald green, bright green, olive green	rose quartz, pink tourmaline, chrysophase, pink danburite, peridot, green fluorite, green aventurine, green citrine, jade
turquoise blue, light blue, blue-green, bright blue, powder blue, royal blue	turquoise, lapis lazuli, aquamarine, blue lace agate, celestite, blue sapphire, sodalite, aqua aura
deep purple, purple blue, dark lavender	amethyst, iolite, azurite, purple fluorite lilac kunzite, electric blue obsidian, sugilite, blue chalcedony
pale lilac, lavender, violet, clear, snow white, translucent	purple jasper, purple sapphire, lilac danburite, labradorite (spectorolite), clear quartz, apophyllite, diamond

HEALING WITH CRYSTALS

Laying crystals on or around the body for healing is a wholly intuitive process, but there are certain principles to keep in mind when you use this technique. The point of healing with crystals is to either draw in or expel positive or negative energy. The specific type of energy required to do this is provided by the crystal, and the placement of your choosen crystal determines where the energy will be focused.

It is really a matter of common sense deciding whether your chief need is to expel negative energy or to absorb positive energy – usually, healing requires a combination of the two. For example, if you are dealing with depression, you will want to drain the negative feelings of worthlessness, but you need to replace those with joy or wholeheartedness.

Single- or double-terminated crystals are specially effective for directing energy to or from the body. If you want to use only one healing crystal, a single- or double-terminated clear quartz may well be sufficient.

WORKING WITH PARTNERS

You may find that working together with someone else achieves better results for you. One of you acts as the healer and the other as the subject. Not everyone can heal, and it is sometimes surprising to find out who is a natural.

Wands
Many crystals come in the shape of a wand. These may be naturally occurring or man-made. Wands are said to be particularly effective for focusing and directing energy like a laser beam.The most versatile wand is quartz crystal.

There are certain measures you must take to deal with the powerful energies that you encounter during a healing session. Both the healer and the subject should make sure that they are well grounded (see Grounding pages 48–49), and are feeling centred and calm before starting a session. The healer should simply see themselves as a channel for energy – the mind and emotions should feel quite neutral. If you are too emotionally involved in the session, things could go wrong.

Most healers feel light pouring in through the top of their head and out through their hands when they are working. To achieve this, meditate beforehand, focusing on opening your crown chakra (see pages 82–83) and allowing the energy to flow in – the energy may only start to flow when you begin the session. For an experienced person this may only take a moment.

It is most important that you do not retain or absorb any negative energy from the subject. After you have finished a session, make sure you do a grounding visualization that expels bad energy. Try visualizing a red cord from your feet that connects you to the centre of the earth. Send all the bad energy down the cord and imagine it as black waste. When the cord returns to a ruby red colour, you have discharged all the energy.

If you feel there are a few areas of weakness in your aura's outer membrane, try taking a fluorite crystal or wand and stroke the areas of your aura that need healing. Do this standing up, then focus and meditate on your aura.

Traditionally used for its healing, cleansing, and neutralizing properties, blue lace agate (pictured above) is also used as a suitable eye elixir for eye strain and aching eyes.

Crystals that should not be used in elixirs:

Some crystals contain toxic material, so you should check to make sure your crystal is safe to use. The following do not work well as elixirs:

- Halite
- Selenite
- Lapis lazuli
- Malachite
- Turquoise

LIQUID CRYSTALS

Gem or crystal elixirs are easy to make, and you may find that they are an effective way of absorbing a particular crystal's vibrations. You can either ingest them, drop a very minute amount on the affected spot, or add them to your bath water. Some practitioners swear by them, but there's not much evidence that their effect is anything other than psychological. Some Ayurvedic astrologers regularly prescribe elixirs as a kind of gemstone remedy. Try them out and see if you can feel any effect.

MAKING AN ELIXIR

Put the crystal in a glass of mineral or spring water, and leave it to stand in the sun for all the hours of daylight of one day. Remove the crystal and pour the elixir in to a dark glass bottle with an airtight stopper.

Use seven drops of the elixir three times a day on the affected spot or add a dash to your bath water. Alternatively, dilute the seven drops of elixir in a glass of water; be sure that your crystal is non-toxic.

BATHING IN CRYSTALS

A delicious way of absorbing crystal vibrations is by taking a bath with crystals. Put your crystal under the tap as you are running your bath, get in, close your eyes, and relax. Try to meditate a little, clearing your mind and allowing the crystal's energy to flow around and through you.

Some people swear by the effects of crystal elixirs in their bath water. Try some yourself and see if they work for you....

WORKING WITH COLOUR

Much theory about how crystals affect us is simply based on their hue, therefore an understanding of colour will help you make sense of the whole field. So if you want to go on to experiment with crystals, it's important to have an understanding of the effects of colour on you and anyone you may work with.

Understanding the influence of the different colours will enhance your healing powers enormously – and help you to make accurate decisions about which crystals to use.

Remember that colour therapists find that although there may be certain general rules with colours, each person has an individual reaction.

Colours do have overlapping meanings. For example, blue promotes self-expression and therefore communication, whereas yellow helps more general interaction with other people. You must use your common sense to decide whether to concentrate on one or several different colours at any one time.

As well as taking colour into account when you are choosing which crystals to use for a healing, try lying on a cloth of a particular colour when you are practising a therapy. As you develop your crystal collection, try to have at least two crystals in each colour range, as you may find certain crystals work more effectively for specific problems.

Basic colour crystal set

Colour	Sample crystals
Red	Carnelian, red jasper
Pink	Rose quartz, pink tourmaline
Orange	Amber, citrine
Yellow	Agate, yellow jasper, amber, citrine
Green	Aventurine, malachite, moss agate
Blue	Blue lace agate, turquoise, sodalite
Purple	Amethyst, fluorite, alexandrite
Black/Brown	Obsidian, onyx, smoky quartz
White/Colourless	Quartz, opal, moonstone

The effects of colour

White: Purifying, cleansing, enlightening, clarifying, and neutralizing.

Red: Physically stimulating, sexually arousing; encourages action, energy, lust, passion, and strength.

Pink: Sympathy, love, and harmony.

Orange: Creatively stimulating; encourages joie de vivre and a sense of well-being; good for the sex organs, fertility, and confidence.

Yellow: Mentally stimulating; enhances sense of personal power, validation and self-worth; counters depression; helps digestion and communication.

Green: Healing, love, and harmony; emotional and physical detox; helps with emotional connection to others; de-stressing; stimulates the liver.

Blue: Relaxation, tranquillity, and calm; helps with the balance of chemicals in the body; stimulates the kidneys and bladder.

Purple/Violet: Peace; clairvoyance, intuition, and spiritual matters; brain activity; cleanses lungs and skin.

Black/Brown: Absorbing negative energy; connection to earth energy; elimination of pain.

CRYSTALS AND THE CHAKRAS

Eastern traditions such as yoga, Buddhism and Hinduism teach that in addition to a physical body, you have an energy body. Balancing the flow of life energy through the channels and centres of your energy body is said to improve your physical and emotional health and your spiritual wellbeing.

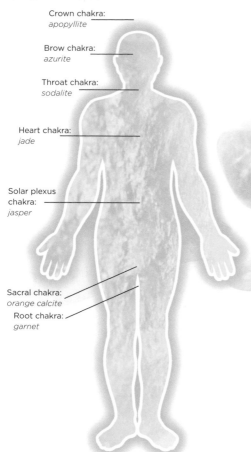

Crown chakra:
apopyllite

Brow chakra:
azurite

Throat chakra:
sodalite

Heart chakra:
jade

Solar plexus
chakra:
jasper

Sacral chakra:
orange calcite

Root chakra:
garnet

A crystal's colour decrees the chakra with which it is associated.

ENERGY HEALING

Energy healing, which includes crystal therapy, is based on the idea that you can regulate your life energy by bringing attention to the body's seven energy centres, called the *chakras*. The chakras are swirling wheels of life energy aligned along the body's main energy channel, running parallel to the spine. Each chakra vibrates at a particular colour frequency and influences a particular set of physical, emotional and spiritual concerns.

USING THE CHAKRA CHART

Many of the techniques in this book are based on pairing crystals with the chakras. The chart opposite shows the location of the chakras and the life issues and potential problems associated with each. You'll find the body parts influenced by each chakra and the potential health problems related to each on pages 70–71. Studying these charts can help you determine which of the crystal techniques in this book best targets your concerns.

CHAKRA CHART

Chakra (colour)	Life issues	Potential problems
Root (red)	safety and security, provide for life's necessities, stability and grounding, the ability to stand up for yourself, good judgement, self-worth	depression, feeling spacey and ungrounded, a lack of self-confidence, low self-esteem, risk-taking, addictions, fears and phobias, suicidal thoughts
Sacral (orange)	flexibility, the ability to enjoy sexual pleasure, the ability to generate new ideas, the ability to nurture and be nurtured	rigidity, lack of desire and sexual satisfaction, fear of touch and intimacy, self-abuse, self-neglect, blocked creativity, shame
Solar Plexus (yellow)	trust, power, prosperity, will, drive, ambition, the responsibility for making decisions, sensitivity to criticism, gut feelings	fatigue, lack of ambition, anger, a tendency to blame others, resentment, guilt, over-sensitivity to criticism
Heart (green or pink)	the ability to love and be loved, hope, empathy, acceptance, forgiveness, the ability to grieve	hatred, loneliness, self-centred, bad relationships, passive-aggressive, jealousy, bitterness, co-dependence
Throat (blue)	personal expression, the ability to speak and to listen, integrity, creative and artistic self-expression, wit and humour	poor communication skills, unwillingness to listen, the inability to express creative ideas, lying and exaggeration
Brow (indigo)	inspiration, intuition, intelligence, memory, vision, insight, wisdom	lack of clarity, lack of perception, can't see the truth, won't learn from experience
Crown (violet or white)	faith, inspiration, spirituality, values and ethics, selflessness, devotion, mystical understanding, enlightenment	confusion, arrogance, the inability to perceive the larger pattern, spiritual doubt, soul loss

UNDERSTANDING CRYSTAL HEALING

Chakra testing

If you are working with another person, you can try muscle-testing using the appropriate crystal to check the health of each chakra. There are two other simple techniques you can also try:

• Touch. If you are working with someone else, see if you can feel her chakras. It is easier if the subject stands, but this also works lying down. Take a few breaths and feel yourself grounding. Focus on your own hands and feel them warm up.

Start to move them very slowly up and down about 8 cm (3 in) away from the other person's body. At each chakra you should be able to feel warmth or coolness, strength or weakness (see above).

• Visualization. Sit as if you are about to meditate and close your eyes. When you feel relaxed, visualize each chakra in turn, and check it with your mind's eye. Check for colour, size, speed of spin, and whether its edges are fuzzy or smooth.

UNDERSTANDING CHAKRAS

The basis of much crystal healing is an understanding of the chakra system that is used in traditional Indian Ayurvedic medicine. The chakras, 'wheels' in Sanskrit, are spinning balls of energy within your body. Like Chinese medicine, Ayurvedic medicine is based on the idea that we should be pulling in fresh, clean energy and expelling negative, used-up energy. The chakras are like a series of cogs running up your spine, continuously renewing your energy.

In a well-balanced and healthy person, the chakras are spinning rapidly and smoothly, and if you visualize them their colours are fairly clear – they should be about the same size as a grapefruit. When someone is mentally, emotionally, or physically unwell, the chakras start to spin either too fast or too slow; they discolour or fragment; enlarge or contract.

Most of us have some chakra misalignment most of the time – after all nobody's perfect. The aim of healing using the chakras is to get the system working more smoothly and evenly.

There are seven main chakras, although many people claim there is an eighth above the crown chakra. There are also smaller chakras in other parts of the body. For healing, the most important of these minor chakras are those located in the hands, since these are connected to the heart chakra – you should be very aware of them if you are healing someone else. There are also two small ones in the feet connected to the root chakra. Being aware of these chakras will help you to stay grounded during your healing sessions.

Chakra Cleanser
A simple but effective crystal layout for the chakras is to put one single-terminated crystal above your head pointing downward and one at your feet pointing upward; visualize energy running smoothly between the crystals up and down through your chakras.

THE SEVEN CHAKRAS

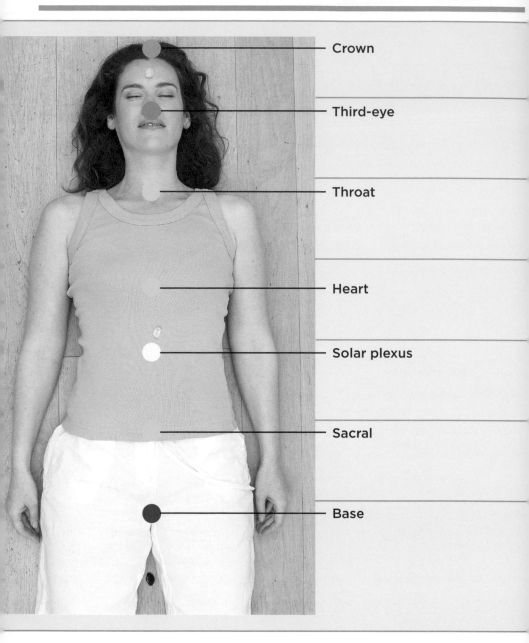

Crown

Third-eye

Throat

Heart

Solar plexus

Sacral

Base

Colour: Violet **Benefits:** Spiritual enlightenment, connection to the source	**Associated sense:** Transcendence **Crystals:** Mainly clear, violet **Examples:** Diamond, clear quartz, amethyst
Colour: Indigo **Benefits:** Second-sight, clear thinking, knowledge, intuition, wisdom	**Associated sense:** Sixth-sense **Crystals:** Mainly purple, dark blue **Examples:** Lapis lazuli, sodalite, amethyst, fluorite
Colour: Blue **Benefits:** Communication, openness to receiving as well as giving information, self-expression	**Associated sense:** Hearing **Crystals:** Mainly blue **Examples:** Aquamarine, turquoise, celestite, blue lace agate, sapphire
Colour: Green **Benefits:** Love, relationships, sharing	**Associated sense:** Touch **Crystals:** Mainly green, pink **Examples:** Jade, aventurine, watermelon tourmaline, rose quartz
Colour: Yellow **Benefits:** Sense of self, boundaries, assertiveness, will, taking action	**Associated sense:** Sight **Crystals:** Mainly yellow, gold **Examples:** Yellow amber, lemon citrine, sunstone, malachite
Colour: Orange **Benefits:** Creativity, fertility, making manifest	**Associated sense:** Taste **Crystals:** Mainly orange, gold, amber **Examples:** Orange amber, golden topaz, moonstone, carnelian, orange citrine
Colour: Red **Benefits:** Connection to the earth, survival instinct	**Associated sense:** Smell **Crystals:** Mainly red, mauve, brown and black **Examples:** Agate, bloodstone, tiger's eye, hematite, onyx, obsidian, carnelian, sardonyx

REBALANCING THE CHAKRAS

If you could see your chakras, as some energy healers do, each one would appear as a rotating wheel of coloured light, perhaps 7–12 cm (3–5 inches) in diameter. When your body, your emotions and your spiritual nature are all in harmonious balance, your chakras are aligned vertically and all are about the same size. Each chakra also displays its own clear and characteristic colour.

USING YOUR INNER SIGHT

Though you may not be able to see your chakras with your physical eyes, you can use your intuition to sense them. When you feel unwell or your emotions are out of control, turn your attention within and see what you can sense about your chakras. Focus your inner sight on each chakra in turn, starting with the root chakra.

If you sense a variation in the size, spin or colour of one of your chakras – for instance, a throat chakra that is pale rather than vivid blue, or a solar plexus chakra that has too little energy or seems to be spinning too slowly – use the colour balancing technique below to strengthen the chakra's energy.

Exercise: Chakra colour balance

As you have learned, each chakra spins at the frequency of one of the colours of the light spectrum. Crystals that vibrate at a similar colour frequency can help to regularize the chakra's spin and bring it back into alignment. You can also use this technique if you feel the need to strengthen a chakra's emotional or spiritual qualities.

1 Consult the chakra chart on pages 70–71 and choose a crystal that corresponds in colour to the chakra that you wish to strengthen.

2 Sit comfortably cross-legged on the floor or on a chair with your feet flat on the floor. Be sure that your back is straight.

Breathe gently and smoothly in a regular rhythm.

3 Hold the crystal you have chosen in your hands. Visualize the coloured light and energy of the crystal radiating out and flowing into your chakra, balancing and strengthening its energy. Hold for 5–10 minutes.

Ancient oriental cultures have believed in the chakras – internal energy forces in the human body that link inextricably with those of nature – for many centuries. There are a number of crystals that can enhance and develop that invisible connection.

Exercise: Full Chakra Cleanse and Balance

You can also use crystals to cleanse and balance all of your chakras at once. Though this exercise suggests specific crystals for each chakra, feel free to substitute other crystals of the appropriate colours that feel intuitively right to you.

Gather the following crystals or others of your own choosing:
one tumbled smoky quartz (below your feet); one tumbled red jasper (root chakra); one tumbled fire opal (sacral chakra); one tumbled sunstone; (solar plexus chakra); one tumbled green aventurine; (heart chakra); one tumbled turquoise (throat chakra); one tumbled azurite with malachite (brow chakra); one tumbled amethyst (crown chakra); one tumbled clear quartz (above your head).

1 Lie down on a yoga mat or folded blanket. Place a flat pillow under your head to ease tension in your neck.

2 Before you put the crystals in place, consider for a few moments your motivation for engaging in this process. For instance, remind yourself that you are more than just your physical body and your consciousness. You also have an energy body that influences your physical health, your emotions and your spirituality. Because you want your life to be full, vibrant and satisfying, you are taking this time to focus on cleansing, balancing and healing your energy body.

3 As you place the crystals as indicated above, starting with the smoky quartz below your feet, remind yourself that the light and energy of each crystal is working in harmony with the energy of your own chakras.

4 Leave the crystals in place for at least 20 minutes. Remain relaxed and alert. Focus your attention on each chakra in turn, starting with your root chakra and working your way up to the crown. Feel that the energy of the crystal is clearing blockages in your energy pathways and regulating the chakra's size and spin.

5 When you feel ready, gather up the crystals, starting with the clear quartz above your head and working downwards to the smoky quartz below your feet. Gently roll to one side and stand up slowly, feeling that your feet are firmly on the ground and that your life energy is harmonious and balanced.

HEALING YOUR AURA

If you find chakras a hard concept to swallow, then you may need to take a deep breath before you start even contemplating cleansing your aura. The fact is most people, no matter how hard they try, are never going to see an aura – so it's a little hard to believe they exist.

However, surprisingly enough, most people can feel an aura quite easily, given the right circumstances. Once you have felt an aura or two, it is much easier to start visualizing them in your mind's eye, and whole new worlds will open up to you.

The aura is an energy field around a person's body. There are basically four layers to it, but they are rarely clearly demarcated – the layers tend to blend into each other. True clairvoyants can often see all the layers of an aura and the chakras, too. The 'physical aura' is simply the warm energy field around a person – and anyone should be able to feel that without trying. Think about when you shake hands or stand close to someone.

Crystals for auras

- **Amethyst** – draws in spiritual energy, heals holes, cleanses

- **Apache tear** – protects

- **Bloodstone** – cleans rapidly

- **Fluorite** – strengthens aura's membrane, creating a shield

- **Green tourmaline** – heals damaged aura

- **Jet** – protects

- **Magnetite** – strengthens

- **Quartz** – cleanses, protects, energizes

- **Smoky quartz** – cleanses, grounds negative energies

Visualizing your aura

- Relax, clear your mind, and breathe calmly. Close your eyes.

- Now imagine your aura. You may find that it is full of many colours and not layered at all. You may see swirls or clouds like coloured gas.

- Allow the colours to come and go.

- See if you can see the outer membrane of your aura. It may be like a big, rainbow-hued soap bubble.

Bloodstone is a particularly effective crystal for healing auras as its main property is the ability to clean rapidly.

Aura layers: The layers of a person's aura usually blend into each other. The layer of warm energy right next to the body is often visible as white light, but other parts of the aura are more often invisible to the naked eye.

Practise feeling an aura with your partner or a close friend.

FEELING AN AURA

The outer layers are harder to feel separately, but on the very outside of the aura, there is a thin skin, like a membrane. This skin should be smooth and without holes, since it is what protects the person from too much negative energy. Auras typically develop tears and holes when a person is feeling disturbed, and crystals are used to repair these holes as you would patch a damaged tent.

You need to do this exercise with another person, when you are both feeling relaxed and comfortable. Both of you should follow the directions for relaxation before you start.

- Sitting or standing, relax completely. With your eyes closed, work through your body from top to bottom, making sure each muscle is released.

- Check your breathing. Make sure you are breathing – quite gently – to the very bottom of your lungs. Try doing this by focusing on breathing right down into your lower back.

- Take about ten cycles of inhaling and exhaling. Don't gasp for air.

This should be gentle and the flow of air smooth.

- As you breathe, you should find that your mind is clearing of all thoughts. Try to simply concentrate on your breath in order to give your brain a rest.

- When you are ready, open your eyes and stand up. Your partner should also be standing and feeling relaxed. Your partner may want to keep his or her eyes closed, just to test the results of this experiment.

- Slowly start to walk towards your partner with your hands outstretched, but relaxed. Be fully aware of yourself and your partner.

- About 1 m (3 ft) from your partner, you will feel slight resistance. Stop there and feel up and down. You will feel a wall of energy almost like a membrane around your partner – and he or she should feel you touch it too.

- Try this experiment a few times and you will find that it comes quite easily. You will also find that you can visualize the colours of a person's aura more easily now when you shut your eyes.

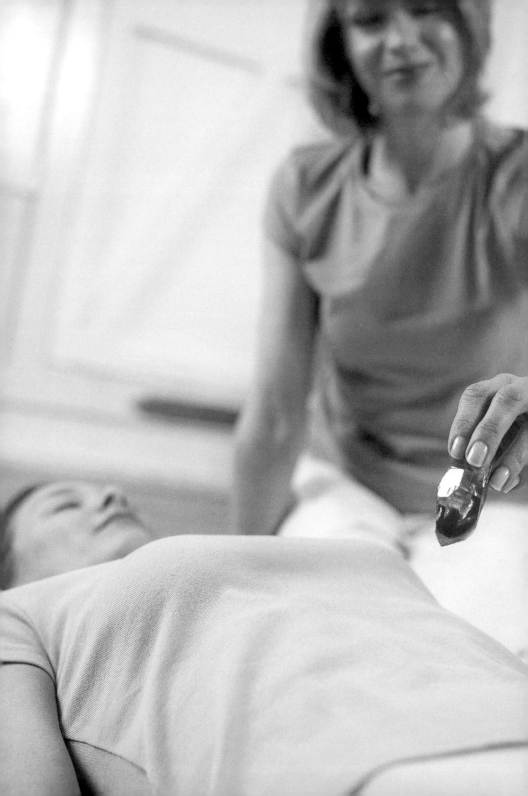

SPECIFIC CRYSTAL HEALING

No one is quite sure how crystals work with the human body – whether the effect is psychological or physical or perhaps some even more mysterious connection. What is sure is that for some people, crystals laid on the body have a beneficial effect. In the West, the art of crystal healing is in its infancy. It is intuitive and there are no set rules, so you should view all your efforts as experiments. Take notes to remind yourself of what works and what does not. Furthermore, take any very rigid advice on which crystals you should use with a pinch of salt – it may just not work for you.

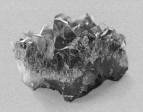

LAYOUTS AND CRYSTALS FOR INDIVIDUAL CONDITIONS

Crystal healing works best when it is focused on alleviating emotional distress, chronic blockage or excess of energy, or an illness that might have a psychological basis. Crystals are not a cure for acute conditions, although they can help to alleviate pain.

All the layouts included in this chapter should be left for at least 15 minutes. They are designed so that you can use them on yourself without having to involve anyone else. Feel free to adapt them in any way that you feel is suitable. When placing crystals around the body, put them about one handspan away from it. Crystals can become more powerful if they are used repeatedly for the same purpose. To begin your therapy, here are two good, all-round layouts for beating stress and detoxifying your body.

Beating stress

It's true that many of us respond well to stressful situations, often needing a certain amount of tension to perform at peak level. However, we need to learn how to manage our stress levels and how to keep them at a comfortable level. This layout is designed to help you wind down, so it is good to come back to it regularly.

• Place one apophyllite on the solar plexus. This is a real healer's crystal that absorbs stress and rebalances energy.

• On the base chakra place one obsidian, black tourmaline, or another black crystal. This will help to absorb negative energy.

• Position one lapis lazuli on the forehead to create calm. Alternatively, fluorite placed here will help the body to reorganize its energy flow.

• If you feel the stress has built up in a particular area of the body, place two single-terminated clear quartz crystals near to the affected area, and pointing outward from either side of your body.

Detox

Green stones are particularly associated with detox. Often they work by helping to stimulate liver and kidneys, which eliminate waste. You may want to try this layout in combination with a detox programme.

- Place one or more peridot crystals where the legs join the torso – this is one of the best detoxing stones. Try moving it around the body to find the spot where you can feel its effects

most. This might be somewhere competely different.

- Place one single-terminated clear quartz on the solar plexus pointing downwards.

Alternative detox crystals:
- Azurite
- Chrysoprase
- Emerald
- Green jasper
- Green opal
- Green tourmaline
- Magnesite
- Malachite
- Turquoise

Peridot

Emerald

Green opal

Green tourmaline

Turquoise

PAIN RELIEF

Pain anywhere in your body is a message that something is wrong. The discomfort may be due to a physical illness or it may reflect emotional or spiritual distress. Crystal healing is most effective when you take the time to investigate all possible reasons for your discomfort, keeping in mind that the cause may be a combination of factors.

EXPLORE THE CAUSES

If you have frequent headaches, for example, start by consulting the crystal healing chart on pages 70–71. Headaches are related to the brow chakra and may result from physical problems with your eyes or your sinuses. Ask yourself: Do I have eyestrain from staring too long at a computer screen? Are my sinuses congested because of a cold or an allergy?

Clear quartz

QUARTZ HEALING FOR PAIN

Quartz is the most effective and versatile crystal pain-reliever. In Chinese medicine, clear quartz is

Smoky quartz

considered to contain the pure essence of chi or life-force. It concentrates the light-filled life energy of sunlight, which radiates through the body as the seven colours of the light spectrum associated with the chakras.

Because it can affect every chakra, a quartz crystal can be used to relieve any kind of pain. Smoky quartz crystals melt away energy blockages and draw off and absorb the excess or blocked energy that may be contributing to the pain or discomfort. Clear quartz crystals release their concentrated natural life-force energy to revitalize and restore balance.

Exercise: Quartz pain relief

For this technique you will need one smoky quartz crystal with a single termination point and one clear quartz crystal with a single termination point. As you recall, single-point crystals focus energy or draw it off, depending on which way the point is facing.

1 Lie down on a yoga mat or folded blanket or sit comfortably on the floor.

2 Hold the smoky quartz crystal in your left hand with the termination pointing away from the painful area. Move the crystal in a small circle just above the painful area in an anticlockwise motion. As you circle the crystal, breathe into the painful area, carrying with your breath the intention to release the pain. In your mind's eye, imagine the crystal is a sponge drawing off and absorbing any painful or blocked energy.

3 When the pain has decreased, switch hands and crystals. Hold the clear quartz crystal in your right hand with the termination pointing towards the area being healed. Move the crystal in a small circle just above the area in a clockwise motion. As you circle the crystal, imagine that the crystal is releasing natural life-force energy to revitalize and restore your body's optimum energy balance.

4 Be sure to wash your hands and cleanse the crystals thoroughly after use.

Healing a headache

As the crystal healing chart on pages 70 and 71 shows, amethyst is a powerful healer for ills influenced by the brow chakra. Chronic headaches, including migraines, tend to respond better to Technique 2, outlined below.

Technique 1

1 Lie down on a yoga mat or folded blanket. Place a flat pillow under your head to ease any tension in your neck.

2 Place a small tumbled amethyst crystal on your forehead as near as possible to the spot where you feel the pain.

3 Close your eyes and follow your breathing all the way in and all the way out. Relax your muscles, starting with your feet and working your way up your body. Pay special attention to relaxing any tension that you may feel in your mouth and jaw. Allow about 20 minutes for the crystal to do its work.

4 Be sure to cleanse the amethyst after use (see pages 54–57).

Technique 2

In Step 2, place a small amethyst crystal with a single-termination point under your head at the base of your skull, with the termination point towards your feet. Follow the other steps as for Technique 1.

A raw cluster of amethyst, mined in Uruguay.

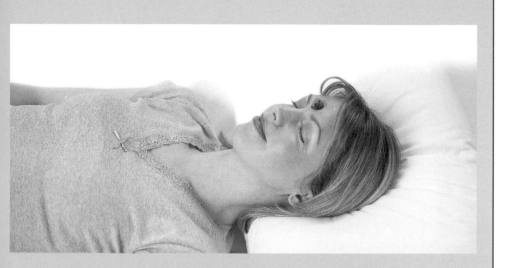

Lie back with the amethyst carefully positioned around your brow chakra and relax, allowing the crystal to disperse the cause of your headache.

Two examples of amethysts in a cut and polished state. The crystal will work effectively for healing a headache, whatever its state of originality or preservation.

Exercise: Steam inhalation for nasal congestion

Inhaling steam infused with a gem essence can relieve the stuffy nose and sinus congestion of a cold or flu. Letting go of feelings by writing about them in your journal, putting on music and dancing them out or simply allowing yourself to cry can also help relieve any congestion. For this technique you will need a small piece of sodalite or blue lace agate.

1 Make a gem essence with a sodalite or blue lace agate crystal.

2 Half-fill a bowl with boiling water. Pour the gem essence into the bowl.

3 Bend over the bowl and cover your head with a towel.

4 Breathe in the gem essence-infused steam deeply through your nose for several minutes. If you are nursing a cold or flu at home, it's fine to repeat this technique up to five times a day.

5 In the evening, pour more of the gem essence into your bathwater and relax as you inhale the healing steam.

COLDS AND FLU

The nasal congestion you get with a common cold and the fever, sore throat and cough of flu are generally caused by a respiratory virus. Though crystal therapy cannot prevent you from catching a cold or the flu, it can help to alleviate your symptoms and make you more comfortable. Of course, you should also follow medical advice, including getting plenty of rest and drinking hot tea and other liquids to keep your body hydrated while it heals.

LISTEN TO THE MESSAGES

As with any crystal healing technique, paying attention to the messages your symptoms may be communicating can make your self-healing more effective. Unrelieved tension and stress and unhealthy lifestyle habits can weaken your immune system and make you more vulnerable to catching a cold or flu virus. Ask yourself: What are the sources of stress in my life and what can I do to minimize them? Am I getting enough rest and exercise? Is my diet healthy?

Blue lace agate

You'll find crystal healing techniques for strengthening your immune system and relieving your tension and stress elsewhere in this book (see pages 94 and 114–115).

Inhaling gem essence from a bowl of steaming water is a great way of cleansing your sinuses and potentially dealing with headaches and facial pain.

TREATING A FEVER

Fever is a sign that your body is fighting an infection. Though having a fever may make you feel uncomfortable, it is actually part of your body's defences. When a virus or bacterial infection enters your body, your white blood cells release a substance that stimulates part of the brain to raise your body temperature. By heating itself up, your body slows down the growth of bacteria and viruses, making it easier for your immune system to eliminate them.

In addition to the crystal healing techniques below, follow medical advice to treat a fever: drink plenty of fluids to prevent dehydration, eat lightly and only if you feel like it, and consult your doctor if your fever is 103 degrees of more or if it persists for longer than 72 hours.

Fever can make you feel terrible, causing headaches and facial flushing. Rehydration and crystal healing will work wonders.

Drinking plenty of water is advisable for many medical conditions, but particularly fever. It is vital to rehydrate properly.

Exercise: Crystal Therapy to Lower a Fever

For the techniques below you will need a small piece of blue chalcedony.

Technique 1

1 Lie down on a yoga mat or folded blanket. Place a flat pillow under your head to ease any tension in your neck.

2 Place the crystal on the site on your body where you are experiencing the greatest heat. Alternatively, place the crystal between your eyes, at the site of the brow chakra.

3 Leave the crystal in place for 20 minutes. It's fine to fall asleep with it still in place. You could try using a small piece of tape to keep it from falling off. Be sure to cleanse the crystal after use.

Technique 2

1 Make a gem essence with the blue chalcedony crystal (see page 65 for instructions).

2 Fill a tub with tepid water that's neither hot nor cold to the touch.

3 Add the gem essence to the bathwater. Soak in the tub for ten minutes, being sure to dry off completely with a fluffy towel when you get out. If you are nursing a fever at home, you can repeat this technique every two hours until your fever has been lowered.

Blue chalcedony

CURING A SORE THROAT

As you have learned, the throat chakra, which influences the throat, neck and mouth, vibrates at the frequency of blue light. So the best crystal for ills affecting your throat, such as a sore throat, laryngitis, swollen glands or hoarseness due to a cold or flu, is blue lace agate.

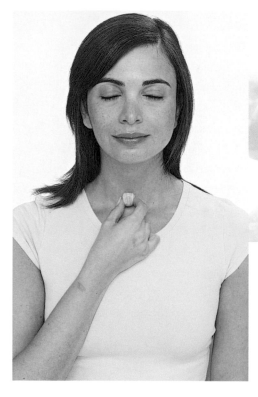

Holding a blue crystal against your throat chakra protects and soothes the throat.

This lovely powdery or periwinkle blue stone, often banded with white lacy threads, harmonizes perfectly with the energy of the throat chakra, activating it to help soothe and calm a painful throat.

BLUE LACE AGATE JEWELLERY

Wearing jewellery made with blue lace agate is both decorative and healing for your throat.

A cabochon is a gemstone that has been shaped and polished. The resulting stone usually has a convex top and a flat back. When it is banded with sterling silver, it makes a beautiful pendant that can be worn on a chain around your neck. To strengthen the energy of your throat chakra and protect against frequent sore throats, wear a blue lace agate cabochon pendant on a 35 cm (14 inch) silver chain, with the flat back of the stone resting against the bare skin at the base of your neck.

Small blue lace agate beads, ranging in size from 5–8 millimetres (¼–¾ in), can also be strung into a lariat necklace that can be wrapped loosely several times around your neck. Sometimes smaller beads of royal blue lapis lazuli are interspersed with the agate, increasing the beauty of the necklace and its healing power.

Exercise: Crystal gargle
For this technique you will need one tumbled blue lace agate crystal.

1 Fill a bowl half-full of spring water.

2 Immerse a cleansed blue lace agate crystal in the water. Place the bowl on the windowsill, preferably overnight, when the crystal can absorb energy from the light of the moon. If that timing is not convenient, set the bowl aside for at least eight hours.

3 Remove the crystal and gargle with the gem essence-infused water. If you are nursing a sore throat at home, gargle with this gem essence every two hours as needed.

Blue lace agate

Exercise: Citrine inner sun meditation

For this meditation, you will need one piece of citrine. A small polished stone, a point or a geode work equally well.

1 Sit comfortably cross-legged on the floor or on a chair with your feet flat on the ground. Be sure that your back is straight. Close your eyes.

2 Hold the piece of citrine with your hands resting comfortably against your abdomen.

3 Breathe slowly and deeply, taking air all the way down to your belly. As you breathe in, imagine that the citrine crystal in your hands is shining like the sun, energizing with its golden light the inner sun of your solar plexus chakra.

4 As you breathe out, imagine that the warming and invigorating energy of your inner sun is spreading throughout your body, strengthening your digestive system, healing its ills and filling you with vitality, warmth and passion.

Envisage your abdominal chakra being suffused with the golden energy emanating from the powerful citrine in your hands.

Citrine

DEALING WITH DIGESTIVE PROBLEMS

Your digestive system includes your oesophagus, stomach and intestines, as well as the organs that produce substances that help break down the food you eat, such as the liver, pancreas and gallbladder. You might think of it as the body's furnace, in which the food you eat is transformed into fuel to power your body's activities.

THE INNER SUN

Digestion is under the influence of the solar plexus chakra, located at the abdomen above the navel. Radiating golden-yellow fire energy, this is like an inner sun, fuelling not only digestion but also your vitality, drive and passion. When it is functioning well, life energy shines outwards from your body's core, helping you get nourishment from both food and life experiences. When it is out of balance, you may feel irritable, angry or resentful and have a tendency to blame others when things go wrong. Not surprisingly, you may also experience stomach aches and other digestive upsets.

Citrine and other yellow crystals carry the power of the sun. Meditating with a citrine crystal can help to strengthen your solar plexus chakra, stimulating digestion, strengthening the bladder and kidneys and relieving constipation and other digestive ills.

Tiger's eye

Golden topaz

INFERTILITY AND REPRODUCTIVE PROBLEMS

Every aspect of a woman's reproductive system functions as a series of cycles. Each month during her childbearing years, an egg matures in an ovary and the uterus prepares a nurturing environment to receive it. If conception does not occur, the blood that lined the uterus in preparation for pregnancy is sloughed off and shed through menstruation.

CYCLES OF LIFE

This monthly cycle is part of the larger cycles of a woman's life. When she enters puberty, her reproductive organs mature, stimulated by the release of hormones. After menopause, menstruation ceases and hormonal changes again trigger natural alterations in the reproductive organs.

Many women experience these cycles as natural and easy. Others have problems with infertility, painful or irregular menstruation,

Regular exercise helps a woman's reproductive cycle work smoothly.

and hot flushes and other uncomfortable symptoms after menopause. Lifestyle choices, including a nurturing diet, regular exercise, maintaining an appropriate weight, avoiding addictions such as smoking and alcohol and reducing stress can help a woman cycle more easily through the natural rhythms of her reproductive life.

When problems do occur, crystal therapy is one of the ways a woman can focus self-healing attention on her natural cycles and rebalance the flow of energy through her reproductive organs.

Exercise: Moonstone rebalancing

For this exercise you will need one tumbled moonstone crystal. Because the monthly phases of the moon mirror a woman's natural cycle, moonstone is nurturing to the female reproductive system, balancing hormones, relieving PMS and other menstrual problems and supporting pregnancy and childbirth.

1 Sit comfortably cross-legged on the floor or on a chair with your feet flat on the floor. Make sure that you keep your back straight.

2 Breathe gently and smoothly in a regular rhythm.

3 Hold the moonstone crystal gently in your hands in front of you.

4 Allow your soft gaze to caress its translucent white or creamy iridescent shimmering curves.

5 Remind yourself that, just like the moon, your reproductive system waxes and wanes in naturally recurring cycles.

6 As the gentle feminine energy of the moonstone rebalances and strengthens, your reproductive processes allow your heart to open in appreciation of the beauty of your own moon-like rhythms.

Exercise: Carnelian energy web

For this technique you will need six clear quartz points with single terminations and a tumbled carnelian crystal.

1 Lie down on a yoga mat or folded blanket. Place a flat pillow under your head to ease any tension in your neck.

2 Place the six quartz points around your body, one above your head, one beneath your feet and two each at the level of your elbows and your knees. The terminations should point away from your body.

3 Place the carnelian crystal on your sacral chakra, situated just below your navel.

4 Relax and focus your attention on the rise and fall of your abdomen as you breathe. Remind yourself that you are a confident and courageous woman. Leave the crystals in place for 20 minutes.

Clear quartz

Carnelian

INFERTILITY

One of the most distressing life crises a woman can experience is the long-term inability to conceive a child.

If the woman and her partner have sought medical help for the condition, they both face a multitude of decisions and uncertainties. But quite often the problem is harder emotionally on the woman, who may feel anxious, depressed, out of control and isolated.

Because infertility has so many possible causes, it's difficult, frustrating and expensive to treat. Perhaps the best way that crystal therapy can help is by providing a safe and natural way to release stress, restore vitality and hope and improve the flow of energy through the reproductive organs.

EMPOWERING THE SACRAL CHAKRA

The reproductive system is under the influence of the sacral chakra. A well-functioning sacral chakra connects you to your feelings and gives you a sense of natural flexibility, flow and balance.

Empowering the sacral chakra through crystals can help a woman achieve motherhood.

Orange-red carnelian empowers the sacral chakra, strengthening your reproductive system. It combats anxiety, doubt and despair, reduces irritability and helps you stay calm, courageous and cheerful, even under difficult circumstances. Traditionally, it is said to stimulate fertility in women and potency in men. The emotional support it provides can help you cope with the ups and downs of fertility treatment or any life crisis.

Clear quartz   *Smoky quartz*   *Carnelian*   *Citrine*

MENOPAUSE

For many women, the menopause signals that a major cycle of life is ending and a new one is beginning. In addition to the physical changes, their children may be leaving home at this time, their love relationships may be shifting or their older relatives may need care. This watershed time is a perfect opportunity to take stock, review the past and consider what you wish to build for the future.

TRANSITION CARE

Physically, menopause impacts on every system of the body. The uncomfortable side effects of the hormonal changes may include hot flushes, vaginal dryness, weight gain, water retention, headaches and sleep difficulties. Emotional symptoms may include mood swings, poor concentration and a loss of interest in sex.

Meditation provides calmness during the turmoil of menopause.

Green fluorite   *Blue lace agate*   *Amethyst*

Crystal therapy can be a useful part of the way a woman takes care of herself during this transition.

Other kinds of loving self-care are also helpful, such as enrolling in a yoga or meditation class, renewing an interest in painting or another form of creative expression and getting enough rest and exercise.

Exercise: Menopause support web

For this technique you will need six clear quartz points with single terminations, one tumbled smoky quartz, one tumbled carnelian, one tumbled citrine, one tumbled green fluorite, one tumbled blue lace agate and one tumbled amethyst.

1 Lie down on a yoga mat or folded blanket. Place a flat pillow under your head.

2 Place the six clear quartz points around your body, one above your head, one beneath your feet and two at the level of your elbows and your knees. The terminations should point away from your body.

3 Place the smoky quartz on your root chakra, the carnelian on your sacral chakra, the citrine on your solar plexus chakra, the green fluorite on your heart chakra, the blue lace agate on your throat chakra and the amethyst on your brow chakra.

4 Leave the crystals in place for 20 minutes. As the crystals rebalance your body, mind and spirit, allow a picture to appear in your mind's eye of yourself in five years, having passed through the menopause, fully engaged in enjoying the next stage of your life.

STRENGTHENING THE IMMUNE SYSTEM

Your immune system helps your body stay healthy. Its interconnected network of glands and organs stimulates the production of lymphocytes, a type of white blood cell that seeks out and destroys disease-causing viruses and bacteria. It also eliminates wastes from the food you eat and the air you breathe.

Tapping your body with a crystal or your fingers stimulates the thymus and the spleen.

If you are prone to colds or find it hard to recover quickly from minor illnesses, your immune system may be functioning poorly. Ignoring your body's needs by getting too little rest, exercise and healthy food can weaken your immune system, as can overwork and stress.

TAPPING

Two important parts of your immune system are the thymus, a butterfly-shaped gland in the centre of your chest, and the spleen, a purplish-red organ on the upper left side of your abdomen. A quick way to stimulate the flow of energy to these organs is by tapping on them.

When you feel stressed or tired, tap firmly in the centre of your chest above the breasts with the four fingers of each hand for about 20 seconds. Then move your fingers down from the thymus, out to your nipples and straight down to the second rib beneath your breasts. Tap firmly with several fingers for about 20 seconds to stimulate the energy pathways that support the spleen. Use an energizing crystal of your choice.

Clear quartz

Aqua aura

Exercise: Immune stimulator

The immune system can also be strengthened with crystal therapy. As you have learned, quartz is a powerful master healer. For this technique you will need one aqua aura quartz point and one clear quartz tumbled crystal.

1 Lie down on a yoga mat or folded blanket. Place a flat pillow under your head to ease any tension in your neck.

2 Place the aqua aura point on your thymus and the tumbled clear quartz crystal in the centre of your forehead.

3 Leave the aqua aura and quartz crystals in place and remain still for 10–20 minutes.

4 Be sure to cleanse both the crystals after you have finished with them.

DETOXIFICATION

Whole grains, dried fruit, nuts and seeds all encourage your body to eliminate waste.

Detoxification means helping your body cleanse itself of the residues of living in the modern world, including toxins from air and water pollution, food additives, cigarette smoke and other environmental hazards. Your body detoxifies itself naturally each time you exhale carbon dioxide from the air you breathe and through the natural processes of elimination. However, taking steps to support your body's ability to detoxify can help prevent and heal illness and encourage vibrant health.

FOOD AND WATER

Eating a diet rich in fibre, including whole grains, pulses, nuts, fruit and vegetables aids the elimination of wastes. Drinking plenty of water – 2 litres (3½ pints) – every day is also helpful. A great morning detox drink to assist your kidneys and liver is a glass of hot water mixed with the juice of half a lemon.

Crystal therapy can also support natural detoxification, strengthening your immune

Regularly eating fruit, such as grapefruit, helps your body in the natural detoxification process.

system. In the technique described opposite, you use a crystal to apply gentle pressure to the palms of your hands. In reflexology, the palms of the hands and soles of the feet are regarded as mirroring the whole body. Stimulating your palms sends energy through the pathways of your body, clearing blockages and encouraging your body to release toxins.

The rubbing application of various crystals to the hands – particularly Danburite – can effect a remarkably cleansing detoxoification process on a variety of bodily organs.

Exercise: Danburite detox

For this technique you will need one natural danburite crystal with a single-termination. A powerful healing stone, generally pink, yellow or lilac in colour, danburite strengthens the liver and gallbladder, supporting detoxification.

Danburite

1 Sit comfortably. Hold the danburite crystal in your right hand.

2 Gently circle the crystal into the palm of your left hand, running the termination point of the crystal over the whole palm from the tips of each finger to the wrist. It's not necessary to push hard or to dig the crystal into your hand. Simply move the danburite over your skin in a rhythmic motion.

3 Then switch the crystal into your left hand and repeat the process, running the crystal over the whole of your right palm.

4 When you have finished, wash your hands and drink at least 250 ml (8 fl oz) of spring water. Also, be sure to cleanse the crystal.

DEALING WITH ADDICTIONS

The immune system can be weakened by addictions to alcohol, food, tobacco and drugs. Addictions not only have negative physical consequences but also bring anxiety, stress, confusion and other psychological and emotional ills.

AMETHYST HEALING

Amethyst is the most useful crystal for helping you to overcome addictions. A stone of the mind, it brings calmness and clarity and promotes sobriety and abstinence. A famous ancient detoxifier, it also helps to balance overworked, overstressed and overwhelmed mental states.

The word 'amethyst' comes from a Greek word, amethustos, which means 'not drunken'. In Greek mythology, Amethyst was a mortal maiden who incurred the wrath of Dionysus, the god of wine. When she cried out to the goddess Artemis for help, Artemis protected the girl by turning her into a pillar of white quartz. When he realized what had happened, Dionysus shed tears of remorse into his wine. The

An amethyst necklace, amulet or bracelt will help protect you from the vagaries of the world.

Amethyst point

goblet spilled and the wine stained the quartz purple. Since that time, purple amethyst crystals have been used in Greece as a means of aiding sobriety. Even today, goblets carved from amethyst are said to prevent drinkers from being overcome by wine and spirits.

Try some of the following more contemporary techniques to focus the healing power of amethyst on your addictive habits:

- Wear an amethyst pendant, ring or earrings to keep the sobering power of amethyst with you during the day. When you put on the jewellery, remind yourself that you love yourself enough to overcome habits that compromise your health and peace of mind.

Jewellery made from amethyst keeps the wearer grounded through the trials of the day.

- Place a small dish of amethyst crystals in your home or on your desk – anywhere where their vibrant purple colour can symbolize the resolutions you've made to change your behaviour.

- Make an alcohol-free amethyst gem essence. Bottle it and splash a little on your pulse points at your wrists and the base of your neck whenever your willpower needs a boost.

- Place an amethyst crystal under your pillow before you go to sleep to put yourself in touch with your feelings and values as you rest.

Tumbled, raw and faceted amethysts

INSOMNIA AND SLEEPING PROBLEMS

Many people have occasional difficulties falling asleep or staying asleep. Sometimes the problem is caused by stress or by practices such as drinking excessive amounts of coffee or alcohol. Working out regularly at the gym, writing in your journal or meditating can help you manage your stress so that it does not stand in the way of a good night's sleep.

A SLEEP DIARY

Keeping a sleep diary can also help you become aware of behaviour patterns that may be disturbing your sleep.

A journal will guide you towards self-knowledge and a deeper understanding of your crystals.

Amethyst

The regular use of crystals can help you restore the good night's sleep that you were once accustomed to.

Every day during a two-week period write down what time you go to bed, what you do before bedtime, what you eat and drink, how long you sleep and other sleep-related information. At the same time, use your journal to keep track of how well the crystal therapy technique described opposite works for you. Review your entries regularly and make changes in your routine to see whether they improve your sleep.

Sodalite

Exercise: Crystal therapy for insomnia

For this technique you will need one tumbled amethyst or one tumbled sodalite crystal. As you have learned, amethyst is a natural tranquilizer that helps to calm and soothe the mind. Deep blue sodalite is especially useful if your sleep diary reveals that nightmares, panic attacks and fears are disturbing your sleep.

Lie comfortably on your back in bed. Place the amethyst or sodalite crystal on your brow chakra. Leave the crystal in place as you practise one of the following relaxation techniques.

Technique 1

Put a hand on your stomach and take long, slow breaths, allowing your belly to expand as you inhale. As you exhale, relax your chest and shoulders. Focus your attention on the rise and fall of your abdomen until you feel that you are completely relaxed.

Technique 2

Allow a picture to arise in your mind of a scene or activity that you find peaceful and soothing, especially an activity with a regular rhythm, such as walking in the woods, swimming or petting your dog or cat. Focus on the repetitive rhythm and relax.

SUMMARY OF HOW TO TREAT COMMON AILMENTS

Crystals should never be a substitute for a doctor's advice, but they can aid cures that you are already using. They are especially effective for chronic conditions such as fatigue.

COMMON AILMENTS

All-round healing
In general green crystals often help the healing process. Specifically, peridot, garnet, rhodonite, and sapphire are good for all round healing and boosting the immune system.

Arthritis
Fluorite placed on the spot or a grossular garnet in a bath.

Asthma
Carry apophyllite with you. During an attack hold it to your chest. WARNING: do not substitute this crystal for any more conventional cures that you are using. This is additional.

Backache
Ask someone to gently stroke the affected area with smoky obsidian or smoky quartz.

Chronic pain
In general, black crystals dissolve pain.

Chronic fatigue
Ametrine, apatite, citrine, green tourmaline, and rutilated quartz are all said to alleviate chronic fatigue. Wear them continuously, and so that they touch the skin – maybe a string of jet, obsidian, or onyx. You should also try a regular layout using crystals that aid digestion.

Eyes
Traditionally, many crystals are associated with curing eye infections and aiding weak eyesight. Aquamarine, beryl, emerald, and blue chalcedony in particular are recommended to help strengthen weak eyes.

COMMON PSYCHOLOGICAL PROBLEMS

Addiction	Amethyst	**Psychosomatic illness**	Pink chalcedony
Anxiety	Chalcedony, opal		
Anorexia	Topaz	**Phobias**	Chrysocolla, citrine, prehnite, sodalite
Depression	See p. 136		
Low self-esteem	Onyx	**Paranoia**	Sugilite
Mood swings	Lepidolite	**Rage**	Aventurine, peridot
Obsession	Green jasper, obsidian	**Shyness**	Rhodonite
		Worry	Amazonite, onyx

Eczema	Lay antimonite on the affected area and focus on the crystal's healing energy.
Headache	Lie in a darkened room with one of the following crystals over your third eye chakra: amethyst, dioptase, emerald, larimar, magnesite, or smoky obsidian.
Indigestion	Agate, antimonite, aragonite, chrysocolla, citrine, epidote, jasper, and topaz are all said to aid digestion. In general, yellow and orange crystals and those associated with the sacral chakra, often have properties that aid the intestines and stomach.
Menopause	Wear moonstone.
Menstrual cramps	Wear chrysocolla, malachite, moonstone, or serpentine – or lay the crystal on your back.
Self-healing	Wear alexandrite, chrysoberyl, or larimar.
Trauma or shock	Malachite, obsidian, or rhodonite on the heart or solar plexus chakras, or wherever you feel it is appropriate.
Wound healing	To hasten post-operative healing wear amber, garnet, obsidian, or rhodonite next to the skin.

CRYSTALS AND YOUR EMOTIONS

Because they work on the mind and body energetically, crystals are especially helpful in overcoming mental and emotional problems. From time to time the flow of life-force through the chakras can become unbalanced and emotional problems may indicate that either too much or too little energy is travelling through a chakra. Your own experience is likely to confirm this idea. Think of how constricted your heart feels when you are lonely or how much fiery energy you feel in your solar plexus when you are angry. Crystals help you to balance the flow of your energy and improve your mental and emotional health.

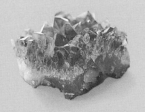

HOW CRYSTALS AFFECT EMOTIONS

As you have learned, the seven chakras correspond to major areas of your life, including your psychological and emotional health. As the subtle electromagnetic vibration of a crystal resonates with the energy of a chakra, it helps to 'tune' the chakra's energy flow, drawing off excess energy or infusing additional energy as needed.

Root chakra – *bloodstone*

Sacral chakra – *orange calcite*

THE CHAKRAS AND THE EMOTIONS

The first step in using crystals for emotional healing is to identify which chakra influences your problem.

THE ROOT CHAKRA influences emotional survival issues. Too little root chakra energy can make you excessively fearful or give you a tendency to feel scattered or ungrounded. Too much energy can manifest in clinging to possessions, people or excess body weight.

THE SACRAL CHAKRA influences sexuality and emotional flow. Too little sacral chakra energy can make it difficult for you to feel emotional or sexual pleasure. Too much energy can make you feel as if you are swinging back and forth between emotional extremes or constantly needing the pleasurable stimulation of parties, partners or sex.

A healthy emotional state means a happy relationship.

THE HEART CHAKRA influences love and relationships. Too little heart chakra energy can make you feel self-centred, lonely or fearful of intimacy. Too much energy can lead to a lack of appropriate emotional boundaries, co-dependence or emotional neediness.

THE SOLAR PLEXUS CHAKRA influences power and will. Too little

Heart chakra - *rose quartz*

Throat chakra – *aquamarine*

Brow chakra – *lapis lazuli*

solar plexus chakra energy can make you feel timid, tired or reluctant to take on power or responsibility. Too much of this energy can manifest in needing always to be in control of others or to feeling constantly angry.

THE THROAT CHAKRA influences the spheres of communication and creative expression. Too little throat chakra energy can make it difficult for you to speak up in groups or to express yourself clearly in writing. However, too much throat chakra energy can lead to talking too much or too loudly, often without saying anything very important.

THE BROW CHAKRA influences perception and intuition. Too little brow chakra energy can make it hard for you to see what's really going on around you or to trust your intuitive perceptions. Too much energy can cause you to have nightmares and difficulty separating reality from illusion.

USING THE CRYSTAL EMOTIONS CHART

THE CROWN CHAKRA influences knowledge and understanding. Too little crown chakra energy can lead to rigid or narrow-minded thinking. Too much energy can cause you to feel detached from the real world and to seem to be always living in your head.

The more you understand about how the chakras affect your emotions, the better you'll be able to use crystals to support your mental and emotional health. The chart opposite gives a basic emotional healing crystal for each chakra. Place the crystal on the chakra and leave it in place for 20 minutes while you relax quietly.

CRYSTALS EMOTIONS CHART

CHAKRA	EMOTIONAL KEYWORDS	HELPFUL CRYSTALS	
ROOT	security, self-esteem, being at home in the world	Bloodstone helps you to feel grounded, protected and secure.	
SACRAL	feelings, intimacy, desire, pleasure	Orange calcite helps you to overcome sexual fears and balance your emotions.	
SOLAR PLEXUS	trust, personal responsibility, courage	Tiger's eye helps you to use your resources to accomplish your goals.	
HEART	love, compassion, empathy, relationship	Rose quartz opens your heart to love and relieves heartache and grief.	
THROAT	loyalty, integrity, self-expression	Aquamarine clears blocked communication and promotes self-expression.	
BROW	clarity, open-mindedness, imagination	Lapis lazuli encourages clear thinking, self-awareness and vision.	
CROWN	self-knowledge, learning, understanding	Apophyllite encourages introspection and supports truthful understanding.	

RELAXATION AND STRESS RELIEF

You've no doubt had days when everything seems to go wrong and your emotional reactions are way over the top. You may be so upset that you can't stop crying, or you may find yourself snapping at your kids or colleagues, or you may feel so worked up that you can barely think straight.

WHAT STRESS DOES TO YOUR BODY

Physiologically, what's happening is that your adrenal glands are secreting a hormone that is spreading throughout your body, raising your blood pressure, speeding up your heart and causing the 'on alert' feeling that is often called the 'fight or flight' response. This natural reaction is your body's way of providing the extra energy that you need to protect yourself from danger. However, when being on stress alert turns into a regular habit, your body's energy reserves become depleted. Over time, you may be at risk of stress-related ailments such as heart disease, high blood pressure, migraines and depression.

Labradorite

RELAXATION CRYSTALS

Crystals can provide an energetic aid to relaxation and stress relief. Because of their soothing and

Moonstone

balancing effect on all levels of your being, they can help your body slow the release of stress hormones, increase your awareness of negative thought patterns and mental attitudes and quieten your emotional responses.

The crystals listed below are among the most useful for relieving stress and promoting relaxation.

- **Amethyst** relieves tension headaches brought on by stress.

- **Bloodstone** grounds your body and reduces irritability and impatience.

- **Labradorite** releases fears and insecurities and calms an overactive mind.

- **Moonstone** calms and balances overreactions by reminding you that whatever happens is part of a natural cycle.

- **Rose quartz** soothes the emotions and helps to slow the release of stress hormones.

- **Tiger's eye** helps to reduce any self-criticism and negative thought patterns that may be contributing to stress.

Stress is bad for you – use your crystals to help you release tension and nervous energy.

Rose quartz

RELIEVING STRESS

The techniques outlined below and on the opposite page will help relieve stress whether you are at home, at work or on the go. One is for emergencies, while the other is a more comprehensive treatment.

Amethyst

Many crystals have a soothing and balancing effect on the body, mind and spirit.

Exercise: Emergency remedy
This quick technique is useful at work or wherever you need immediate relief from tension and stress.

1 Place a small dish of the relaxation crystals listed on pages 130–31 on your desk or kitchen worktop. When you feel stressed, reach into the dish and let your intuition guide you to the appropriate crystal.

2 If possible, sit or lie quietly for several minutes while holding the crystal. Twenty minutes is ideal, but you will find that even five minutes helps. Alternatively, slip the crystal into your pocket and continue with your activities.

Exercise: Crystal pairs

When you have the time for a more comprehensive stress-relieving treatment, try the following technique. It uses a pair of balancing crystals – one that draws out stressful energy and one that fills your body-mind with soothing vibrations. Palm stones – round, flat stones that fit comfortably in your hand – are especially good for this technique, but you can also use small tumbled stones.

You will need a pair of crystals, depending on your situation and need. The first crystal listed in each pair below is the more active and energetic stone. Its job is to relieve stress. The second crystal calms and soothes.

- **Amber and Blue Chalcedony**
  Amber absorbs negative energy, while blue chalcedony promotes acceptance and optimism.

- **Clear quartz and Amethyst**
  Clear quartz relieves pain and tension, while amethyst brings calmness and mental clarity.

- **Tiger's eye and Aragonite**
  Tiger's eye slows the release of stress hormones, while aragonite encourages insight into the causes of your distress.

1 Choose one of the crystal pairs above. Sit comfortably or lie on your back on a yoga mat or folded blanket.

2 Hold the more active crystal (the first crystal in each pair) in your dominant hand (the hand you write with) and hold the calming crystal in your receptive hand.

3 Close your eyes. Consciously relax your muscles, starting with your feet and working your way up your body. Allow about 20 minutes for the crystals to do their work.

Amber

Tiger's eye

CRYSTAL RELAXATION

When you want to unwind after a stressful day, the crystal relaxation web below can help. Setting aside 20 minutes each evening for relaxation using crystals combined with a meditative focus on the breath releases tension in your body and soothes your mind and emotions so that you can get the restoring rest you need.

Exercise: Relaxation web

For this technique you will need one smoky quartz point with a single-termination, one polished labradorite, one tumbled rose quartz, one tumbled aquamarine, one tumbled amethyst and one clear quartz point with a single termination. To get the most benefit from this exercise, you should be private and uninterrupted. Use tape to hold the crystals securely in place if necessary.

1 Lie down on a yoga mat or folded blanket. Place a flat pillow under your head to ease any tension in your neck.

2 Place the smoky quartz crystal under your feet, with the termination pointing away from your body.

3 Place the labradorite on your solar plexus chakra.

4 Place the rose quartz on your heart chakra.

5 Place the aquamarine on your throat chakra.

6 Place the amethyst on your brow chakra.

7 Place the clear quartz just above your head, with the termination pointing away from your body.

8 Now, bring your attention to your breath and imagine that you are breathing with your whole body, from the crown of your head to the tips of your toes.

9 As your muscles relax, imagine your body softening and sinking into the floor. Maintain this state of relaxed awareness for as long as you like. You may need at least 20 minutes to integrate the crystal energies fully.

10 When you have finished, slowly start to breathe more deeply. Stretch your legs and then your arms. Remove the crystals one by one, starting with the top of your head. Then roll over to one side and sit up carefully.

Relax completely as you perform this exercise, and imagine that you are absorbing the crystals into the very core of your being – both body and soul.

ANXIETY AND DEPRESSION

When you are anxious about something, you may feel as if your thoughts are no longer under your control. Your mind circles round and round the same track, repeating a pattern of uneasy thoughts and mental pictures. Persistent worry can negatively impact on your physical health as well as your emotional wellbeing. You may develop headaches and muscle pain, or you may have trouble sleeping. Without relief, you may eventually become depressed.

Each crystal provides a focus for peaceful contemplation.

Cultures around the world have used crystals to release the nervous tension that accompanies worry. Among the most useful are the following:

Amber
Because of its biological origin as fossilized tree resin, golden amber is an excellent natural antidepressant. It both absorbs negative energy and stimulates self-healing. Greek worry beads (see opposite) are traditionally made of amber.

Kunzite
This tranquil pink stone has a mood-lifting effect. It helps to clear stuck emotional energy and to break the worry cycle of obsessive thoughts.

Lepidolite
This calming purple stone soothes emotional distress and helps overcome insomnia. Sometimes called a crystal of transition, lepidolite is also valuable in helping to release old thought patterns.

WORRY BEADS

If you are feeling anxious, you could try following the Greek custom of sliding a strand of smooth amber beads through your fingers to dispel nervous tension and relieve worry. In Greece, these strands are called komboloi, which means 'group of knots'. The custom may have arisen from the knotted strands of prayer beads carried by Greek Orthodox monks. Most worry bead strands have 16–20 beads, with one bead set off and adorned with a tassel. In Greece, you will see the beads being fingered by both men and women.

Amber

Exercise: Worry relief web

For this exercise you will need two natural kunzite crystals and five tumbled lepidolite crystals.

1 Lie down on a yoga mat or folded blanket. Place a flat pillow under your head to ease any tension in your neck.

2 Place one kunzite above your head and one kunzite between your feet.

3 Place the lepidolite crystals on your brow, throat, heart, solar plexus and sacral chakras.

4 Follow your breathing all the way in and all the way out for 20 minutes while the crystals help to discharge the stuck emotional energy of obsessive worry.

Kunzite

Lepidolite

OVERCOMING FEARS AND PHOBIAS

Feeling fearful when you are in actual danger is part of your body's natural self-protection mechanism. Feeling apprehensive before you give a speech or visit the dentist is also natural, so long as you are able to control your fear and keep going. But when fear interferes with your ability to enjoy life fully, it may be a reason for concern.

An intense, irrational fear of a situation or object is called a phobia. Common phobias include fear of closed-in places, heights, tunnels, lifts, water, flying and spiders! Phobias get in the way of daily living by redirecting your life energy towards avoiding the thing you fear. They can also cause physical symptoms, such as stomach cramps or lightheadedness. Untreated, they can lead to addictions and social isolation.

Fear of flying is a very common phobia that can be treated with the help of crystals.

Exercise: Releasing fears and phobias

For this exercise you will need one aquamarine crystal with a single-termination and/or one smoky quartz crystal with a single-termination. Aquamarine (Technique 1 below) brings courage and calms your mind. Smoky quartz (Technique 2 below) helps keep your body grounded in fearful situations. Use either technique or one after the other, depending on your need.

Technique 1

1 Sit comfortably cross-legged on the floor or on a chair with feet flat on the floor. Place the crystals nearby. Close your eyes and follow your breathing all the way in and all the way out until you feel both centred and relaxed.

2 With the fingers of your right hand, tap your breastbone three times between your heart and your throat. This place is the witness point.

3 Hold the aquamarine to your witness point with the termination towards your head. Think about the fear or phobia you want to release.

You may feel tingling or throbbing in your witness point as your mind becomes calm.

Technique 2

In Step 3, hold the smoky quartz to your witness point with the termination towards your lap (downwards). Think about the fear or phobia you want to release. You may feel tingling or throbbing in your witness point as your fear is released and body becomes more grounded and centred.

Exercise: Release and forgiveness

For this technique you will need one apophyllite, amethyst or lapis lazuli crystal. Try all three and see which works best for you.

1   Sit comfortably cross-legged on the floor or on a chair with your feet flat on the floor. Place the crystal you have selected nearby.

2   Bring to mind the image of the person or situation towards which your anger is directed. Say, either in your mind or out loud, why you feel resentment, hurt or anger.

3   Pick up the crystal and hold it in your hands. Say, either in your mind or out loud, that in the past you have felt anger towards this person or situation, but now you are going to do your best to release it.

4   Say, either in your mind or out loud, words of release such as: 'I release my anger and forgive you.' As you do, imagine that the anger is draining away, leaving your mind and body at peace.

Concentrate intently on the crystal as you hold it before you in your hand and use it as a conduit to drain away your anger and resentment.

COOL YOUR ANGER

Anger feels awful. Your face turns red, your heart races and it hurts to breathe. Anger is often hot and raging. It can make you yell or throw things or pound your fist on the table. Hot rage can lead to aggression – everything from terrorist bombings to emotional abuse within the family. But anger does not always look hot. It can also manifest as passive-aggressive behaviour and coldly calculated strategies to get back at someone who has hurt you.

Ironically, anger often hurts you as much as it hurts the person towards whom it is directed. The Buddha described anger as reaching your hand into the fire to pick up a hot coal to throw at someone else. Of course, your hand gets burned first!

Apophyllite

CALMING CRYSTALS

Crystals can help you to release your angry feelings before they cause you damage.

- **Apophyllite** calms and grounds your spirit at the same time as it helps you to see clearly the truth of anger-provoking situations.

Amethyst

- **Amethyst** works like a natural tranquilizer to dispel anger and bring patience and acceptance.

- **Lapis lazuli** opens the throat chakra, allowing you to express any repressed anger that may be blocking your ability to communicate.

Lapis lazuli

CLARITY AND COMMUNICATION

Daily life provides many examples of the close connection between your emotions and your mental processes. On days when you are depressed or your self-confidence is low, your mind may feel sluggish or confused, or it may skip restlessly from one topic to another. It may be hard to focus and you may forget appointments or be unable to finish tasks and meet deadlines. Crystals can help to calm an overactive mind and clear confusion.

Keep a smooth mind-boosting crystal on your desk and hold it whenever you need mental clarity.

CRYSTALS FOR CLARITY

The following crystals will enhance clarity and concentration:

- **Amber** improves memory and encourages you to express yourself creatively.

- **Amethyst** relaxes the mind, helping you to feel less scattered or overwhelmed by all the tasks that you have to finish.

- **Apophyllite** brings balance and releases excessive mental energy.

- **Aquamarine** filters mental information, sharpening perception and aiding clear communication.

- **Bloodstone** enhances stability and strengthens your ability to make decisions.

Exercise: Mind support layout

For this technique you will need one tumbled sodalite, one natural clear quartz, one polished labradorite, one tumbled amethyst and one tumbled or natural smoky quartz.

1 Lie down on a yoga mat or folded blanket. Place a flat pillow under your head.

2 Place the amethyst crystal above the top of your head.

3 Place the sodalite crystal high on your forehead.

4 Place the clear quartz in between your eyebrows.

5 Place the labradorite to the right of your head.

6 Place the smoky quartz to the left of your head and spend 20 minutes lying quietly.

- **Clear quartz** clears mental blockages and aids concentration.

- **Labradorite** encourages clear thinking and rationality balanced by introspection and intuitive wisdom.

- **Lapis lazuli** amplifies thinking, bringing objectivity and clarity to your thought processes.

- **Sodalite** banishes mental confusion so that the mind can take in new information.

Place a mind-supporting crystal on your desk or wear it as a pendant or earrings to encourage clear thinking, concentration and mental harmony throughout your workday. When you feel overloaded, hold a mind crystal in your hands for a few moments. Also try the layout above to enhance memory, focus and learning.

Aquamarine

Labradorite

Sodalite

YOUR THROAT CHAKRA

Blue crystals, including blue lace agate, sodalite, aquamarine and lapis lazuli, support your throat chakra, improving your ability to communicate clearly. It's easy to see that you use the throat when you speak. However, the throat chakra also influences your ability to listen and to communicate in writing and through your gestures and body language.

In addition to communicating with others, the throat chakra also helps you communicate with yourself. Without the self-knowledge that the throat chakra offers, you might become confused by the different signals you receive from your body or be unable to regulate your mental chatter. A well-functioning throat chakra also improves your creativity – your ability to express yourself through poetry, music, dance and the visual arts.

A poorly functioning throat chakra can affect your relationships. You may find it hard to understand what other people are telling you, or you may misinterpret their non-verbal signals, leading to problems at work and with your family and friends.

The throat chakra will benefit enormously from the application of any blue crystal, resulting in improved communication and a better understanding of your relationships.

Energizing your throat chakra

Here are some quick and easy ways to send energy to your throat chakra:

- Warm up your voice by singing in the shower or humming along with a CD or the radio as you drive to work.

- Prepare a gem essence using blue lace agate, sodalite, aquamarine or lapis lazuli. Carry the gem essence with you in a small bottle and dab a little of it on your throat before you need to speak.

- Gently massage your neck and throat area with a blue-coloured crystal to infuse your throat chakra with energy. Alternatively, try wearing a blue-coloured crystal on a short chain, to ensure that your throat chakra is energized throughout the day.

Exercise: Crystal voice warm-up

This simple breathing technique helps to open your throat chakra and relax your voice. You will need one tumbled blue lace agate, sodalite, aquamarine or lapis lazuli crystal.

1 Stand or sit up straight and close your eyes. Hold the crystal you have chosen gently against the base of your throat.

2 Breathe in through your nose and exhale through your mouth.

3 Breathe in more deeply through your nose, expanding your abdomen to allow your lungs to fill fully. Engage your voice as you exhale with a relaxed 'aaah'. Repeat five times.

Blue lace agate

Lapis lazuli

LOVE AND RELATIONSHIPS

Crystals can help you enhance the energy of the two chakras most closely linked to love and relationships: the sacral chakra and the heart chakra. A well-functioning sacral chakra will connect you to your feelings and make it possible for you to enjoy physical pleasure. The heart chakra adds the bonds of love to your relationships.

ENHANCING DESIRE AND SATISFACTION

The sacral chakra governs sexuality. Blockages here can make it hard for you to feel desire. A well-functioning sacral chakra opens you to the joys of touching and being touched, of giving and receiving, of achieving sexual satisfaction and enjoying the sensation of giving satisfaction to others.

Orange-coloured crystals such as carnelian, orange calcite and citrine vibrate with the energy of the sacral chakra, releasing blockages and encouraging the free flow of sexual energy. Carnelian is especially effective for heightening interest in sex, overcoming impotence and strengthening the reproductive organs.

Citrine

Sexual pleasure is experienced through the sacral chakra, which is associated with orange crystals.

Exercise: Sacral pleasure breath

For this technique you will need one or two pieces of orange carnelian, orange calcite or citrine.

Technique 1

1 Prepare a private place to work in that's warm enough for you to be comfortable without clothes. If you wish, use candles, flowers, soft music and pillows to make the space more intimate and relaxing.

2 Take off your clothes and lie down on a yoga mat or folded blanket. Place a flat pillow under your head to ease any tension in your neck.

3 Place the orange-coloured crystal on your sacral chakra, just below your navel.

4 As you breathe in, visualize the air coming in through your nose and travelling down your body, carrying warmth and energy to your lower abdomen. Visualize or feel a vibrant orange glow flowing from the crystal into your sacral chakra, awakening and healing your sexual centre. You should continue the visualization for 5–15 minutes.

Technique 2

You can also use these steps with an intimate partner as a warm-up for lovemaking. Lie side by side, holding hands if you wish. Each partner places a pleasure-enhancing crystal on the sacral chakra and breathes in its energizing orange glow. You will both soon feel very aroused.

Carnelian

Orange calcite

OPENING THE HEART

Rose quartz has a strong energetic connection to the heart chakra. Often called the stone of unconditional love, it encourages healthy self-love, forgiveness and reconciliation and opens the heart to romantic love. Rose quartz is also a comforting stone when you have suffered heartbreak, especially grief over the loss of someone you have loved.

HEALING YOUR HEART WITH ROSE QUARTZ

Try some of the following ways of using rose quartz to open and heal your heart.

- Place a piece of rose quartz under your pillow or hang a rose quartz pendant from your bedside lamp to improve your current relationship or attract new love into your life.

- If you are grieving, prepare a gem essence using rose quartz and add it to your evening bathwater. Lie back in the gem-infused water and allow your heart to be bathed by the crystal's healing vibrations.

- When you need to resolve an interpersonal conflict or mediate a dispute, hold a piece of rose quartz to encourage co-operation, forgiveness and a peaceful resolution of the problem.

Use the meditation described opposite to open your heart to the joys of romantic love.

Rose quartz in the bedroom encourages love and tenderness to flow into your home.

Exercise: Heart rose meditation

This meditation will allow love to flow into your being and open you to all the possibilities of romance. You will need one polished rose quartz crystal carved into the shape of a heart.

1 Lie on your back on a yoga mat or blanket. Place a flat pillow under your head to ease any tension in your neck.

2 Place the rose quartz heart on your heart chakra, between your breasts.

3 Spend a few minutes watching your breath, paying attention to the expansion and contraction of your chest. Listen to your heartbeat.

Rose quartz

4 Bring to mind the image of someone you love or have loved strongly in your life. Appreciate as fully as you can everything that was or is wonderful about this relationship.

5 Now turn your attention to your heart chakra. Visualize it as a beautiful budding rose being warmed by the gentle vibrations of the rose quartz heart. Allow the tender feelings you have for the loved person you are recalling slowly to open the petals of the rosebud until your heart rose is in full and glorious bloom.

Rose quartz bracelet

Use both hands to hold the kunzite crystal close to your heart chakra, where it will do its valuable healing work.

HEALING PAST HURTS

If you have been hurt in your relationships, you may have closed down the flow of energy through your heart chakra to protect yourself from being hurt again. Opening to unhappy memories is sometimes painful, but it is a necessary first step to getting your emotional energy moving again.

The crystal healing meditation opposite combines the energies of three crystals that gently release past hurts and heal and balance your emotions:

- **Amethyst** promotes emotional balance and alleviates feelings of sadness and grief.

- **Blue lace agate** helps to release repressed feelings, dissolve anger and heal feelings of rejection.

- **Kunzite** heals heartache, facilitates introspection and lifts your mood.

Blue lace agate

Amethyst

Exercise: Heartache relief circle

For this technique you will need six tumbled amethyst crystals, six tumbled blue lace agate crystals and one natural kunzite crystal. Sit comfortably on the floor, using a pillow if you wish.

1 Alternate the blue lace agate and amethyst in a circle around you.

2 Hold the kunzite against your heart chakra, using both hands. Bring to mind the past hurt you wish to heal. Imagine or feel that the kunzite is gently drawing out the painful emotional energy of this experience and replacing it with tenderness and compassion for your past suffering.

3 When you feel ready, hold the kunzite away from your body, pointing it outwards beyond the crystal circle. In your mind or out loud, speak words of release, such as 'I release myself from dwelling on the past.' Imagine or feel that your anger and sadness are leaving you and travelling far away.

4 When you feel that this part of the process is complete, place the kunzite on the floor outside the crystal circle. Now imagine that your mind and body are bathed in the healing vibrations of the crystals surrounding

you. Try to absorb this healing energy. In your mind or out loud, say words of comfort and hope, such as 'I open my heart to new possibilities.' As you do, feel that your emotions are calm and balanced and that your mind is at peace.

Kunzite

CRYSTALS FOR HARMONY AND PROTECTION

Because of their unique ability to focus and transmit psychic energy, crystals can strengthen your natural spiritual abilities. A crystal's spiritual power is enhanced by your motivation and intention. If you seek inner balance, crystals can help you align your body's energies. If you wish to create harmony in your environment, crystals can make your home a peaceful sanctuary. Holding a crystal during meditation helps you sharpen your intuition, enlarge your creative vision and deepen your ability to concentrate. Placed under your pillow with intention, crystals can open you to dreams that provide spiritual guidance and personal insight.

CRYSTALS AND YOUR SPIRIT

Crystals have been valued since ancient times as aids to vision, intuition, wisdom and other psychic and spiritual gifts. As you will discover in this chapter, working with crystals can help you develop these qualities in yourself.

YOUR PSYCHIC POWERS

Celestite

Green aventurine

Everyone has natural psychic gifts. You've probably experienced times when a hunch told you what would happen, when you 'just knew' what you had to do, or when a dream gave you insight into a current situation. Crystals do not provide these intuitive abilities; rather, they help you develop and strengthen the skills you already have.

Crystal gazing, or scrying, is the ancient practice of seeking visions by gazing into a reflective surface, such as a crystal ball, a mirror or a pool of water. The crystal ball does not produce the images – they are produced by the mind and projected onto the crystal ball, which acts like a screen. The real picture-making magic is in your mind. It is the same ability that allows you to 'see' an apple in your mind's eye when you hear the word.

As you have learned, the ability to envision and to visualize is influenced by the brow chakra, which also controls intuition and psychic gifts such as clairvoyance,

Scrying is the ancient art of visualizing past, present or future events using a crystal ball.

the ability to 'see' future events or to receive information from a distant location, and telepathy, the ability to communicate with another mind. You'll have the opportunity to use crystals to develop and strengthen these natural psychic gifts later in this chapter.

INNER GUIDANCE

Crystals can also help you strengthen your ability to meditate. Meditation allows you to turn your consciousness inwards and enter a peaceful state of relaxed awareness in which your mind can more easily connect with the divine energies of universal mind. Crystals that open and stimulate the crown chakra – your gateway to spiritual connection – can facilitate this process.

Crystals can also help you focus your intention on your dreams and use them to seek advice and guidance for your life. By stimulating the throat and brow chakras, they encourage vivid dreams and help you use your intuition to decode a dream's symbols and understand its messages.

CRYSTAL SPIRIT CHART

Chakra	Spiritual keywords	Helpful crystals	
Root	steadiness, right livelihood, confidence	Red jasper brings psychic protection and personal empowerment.	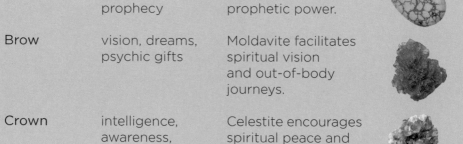
Sacral	going with the flow, good balance, abundance, joy	Fire opal awakens inner fire and encourages the growth of personal energy.	
Solar plexus	perseverance, justice, patience, benevolence	Sunstone increases optimism and spiritual enthusiasm.	
Heart	openness, generosity, peace, equanimity	Green aventurine promotes spiritual growth through compassion.	
Throat	creativity, harmony, prophecy	Turquoise enhances creative vision and prophetic power.	
Brow	vision, dreams, psychic gifts	Moldavite facilitates spiritual vision and out-of-body journeys.	
Crown	intelligence, awareness, wisdom	Celestite encourages spiritual peace and unity with universal wisdom.	

BALANCING ENERGIES

You can also use crystals to balance your internal energies and to harmonize the energies in your surroundings. Placed on your chakras with intention, crystals can help you clear blockages in your energy pathways and bring your internal energies into harmonious alignment. Similarly, you can harmonize the energies in your home or office by using your intuition to place appropriate crystals in various locations.

CRYSTAL SPIRIT CHART

Though you'll find instructions in this chapter for using crystals to develop and support these psychic and spiritual abilities, the chart opposite suggests a basic spiritual crystal for each chakra. To strengthen the qualities listed in the chart, place the crystal on the chakra and leave it in place for 20 minutes while you relax quietly.

Choose carefully the crystals you place on your chakras; they may have a powerful effect.

Red jasper

HARMONY AT HOME

The natural beauty of crystals can enhance the decor of your home or office. Sited with intention, crystals can also harmonize the energy of your environment to suit your activities and match your moods.

Crystals intended for display are generally larger than the crystals you use for personal healing. Large raw crystals, crystal clusters and beautiful geodes, spheres and pillars are especially suitable.

Carefully visualize where each crystal should be placed for maximum impact before positioning them around your home.

CRYSTAL PLACEMENT

This page gives some suggestions for crystal placement. However, your own intuition is always your best guide.

Pay attention to how you feel over a period of several days after putting a crystal in place. Often the crystal itself will 'tell' you – actually by stimulating your intuition – whether the site is appropriate.

BATHROOM

Watery crystals like blue lace agate, aquamarine, moonstone, selenite and pink and watermelon tourmaline are perfect for placing in the bathroom.

Try putting a few polished blue lace agate or aquamarine crystals into your bathwater. As you soak in the bath, allow the crystal energies to relax and soothe your emotions and prompt your intuition to provide insights into issues that may be troubling you. You should feel more comfortable in no time at all.

LIVING ROOM/LOUNGE

Citrine energizes and recharges you, as well as encouraging an attitude of abundance and optimism. Place a citrine cluster or geode in the corner of the room farthest to the back and to the left of the entry door (the 'wealth corner' according to the Chinese art of placement) to support your wish for a happy, successful and prosperous life.

KITCHEN

Since the kitchen is often the heart of the home, green-coloured crystals such as green fluorite, green aventurine, moss agate and jade can enhance its loving and nourishing warmth. Place a selection of green crystals on your kitchen windowsill or use a green marble bowl filled with fruit or vegetables as a kitchen table centrepiece.

Light candles and incense burners to relax your mind and prepare you for a good session with your crystals.

BEDROOM

You have already learned that rose quartz is the ideal crystal for encouraging positive love relationships. Other appropriate crystals for placing in the bedroom include green aventurine, which promotes empathy and stress-free relationships, pink tourmaline, a crystal aphrodisiac that encourages sexual pleasure, and red jasper,

which aids dream recall when placed under your pillow.

OFFICE OR HOME OFFICE

Crystals that combine the colours red and green, such as bloodstone and watermelon tourmaline, are ideal for placing in your workspace. Watermelon tourmaline helps you to understand situations and act with patience, diplomacy and tact. Bloodstone encourages clarity and reduces irritation, aggressive attitudes and impatience.

Once you have located any sources of stress and countered them with the appropriate crystal, it is time to encourage some generally good vibrations into your home. Try a few crystals at a time and see their effect on your household before adding more.

OTHER IDEAS FOR CRYSTAL PLACEMENT

Hanging clear quartz crystals in the window so that they send rainbows of colour into your home is both beautiful and draws in positive energy. To bring in good vibrations try placing a large slice of agate or an amethyst cluster near the front door.

Sugilite

Copper is the metal traditionally associated with the goddess Venus and crystals that contain a trace of it are often remarkably effective at harmonizing vibrations. Try placing copper chalcedony, malachite or, if you are feeling extravagant, azurite malachite in the most used room in the house.

The gorgeous violet crystal sugilite (see bottom left), discovered by Dr Kenichi Sugi in the 1940s, is a lovely thing to have in your main room. It encourages love, attentiveness, and sharing. Emerald is also said to bring domestic bliss and ensure good, long-lasting relationships. Citrine is always good to have around because it has a cheerful vibration, as well as attracting prosperity – place a citrine cluster on your dining room table and watch conversation blossom.

MORE ON TOURMALINE

The tourmaline family of crystals is particularly helpful for establishing harmony. Because the vibrations do not clash, you can have a group of different-coloured tourmalines together. Put them somewhere central, such as a coffee table in the living room or on the kitchen table, if that is the most used room in the house. Brown tourmaline is excellent for family commitment and teamwork;

watermelon tourmaline helps love and friendship blossom; black tourmaline keeps your feet on the ground, dissolves blockages, and protects from negative energy; red or pink tourmaline encourages chit-chat and a relaxed social atmosphere; green tourmaline keeps you open to new encounters and full of the wonders of life; and blue tourmaline helps easy, truthful communications.

COMBATING DISCORD

If your household seems to be suffering from discord, place rhodonite in a central position. These are crystals of reconciliation that help blocked communications to flow again.

Black tourmaline

Fuchsite, which is often difficult to locate, is helpful for dysfunctional families, releasing people from un-healthy roles and unknotting co-dependent situations.

Fuchsite

Green emerald tourmaline

ENHANCE YOUR INTUITION

There's nothing magical about intuition. The human mind is amazingly complex. In addition to dealing with the day-to-day information from your senses, your thinking processes and your emotions, it also encodes memories, fantasies and unconscious thoughts and feelings. Some psychologists estimate that 95 per cent of the contents of the mind are unconscious and beneath the surface of everyday awareness, like an iceberg with its great bulk hidden under the water.

Holding a crystal sphere before you and focusing on it as you concentrate your thoughts is a time-honoured psychic practice.

VOICES AND VISIONS

The 'voices' that you hear and the 'visions' that you see when you go inside to access your intuition are, in fact, part of you. They reflect the understanding you have gained from everything that you have experienced in your life – even things you have forgotten or never consciously knew.

Quietening your everyday mind creates the space for the deep wisdom of your mind to provide inspiration and guidance. Using a crystal sphere as a focus point is a time-honoured method of accessing this wisdom.

PSYCHIC GIFTS

With practice and good intentions, anyone can develop psychic gifts such as clairvoyance and telepathy to some degree. Used with integrity and the proper motivation, these gifts can help you extend your mind and senses beyond the horizons of time and space and discover information that is helpful for you and others.

One of the most powerful crystals for developing your psychic gifts is moldavite. This strange crystal is said to be of extraterrestrial origin. It was formed about 15 million years ago when a meteor collided with Earth in the Moldau river valley in the Czech Republic. Combining the energies of Earth and the heavens, moldavite encourages psychic and spiritual growth.

Exercise: Moldavite journeys

Moldavite can help you journey forwards into the future or backwards into the past. You might journey into your own future to gain insight into the consequences of your current actions or you might journey backwards in time to gain insight into the lives of your grandparents or other ancestors. For this exercise you will need one piece of moldavite.

1 Lie down on a yoga mat or folded blanket. Place a flat pillow under your head.

2 Place the moldavite crystal on your brow chakra.

3 Close your eyes and focus on your breathing for a few moments until you feel relaxed and centred. Clarify your intention. Decide where you would like to journey and what you wish to discover.

4 Allow an image to form in your mind's eye of the place to which you wish to journey. Allow yourself to enter the story, knowing that you can return to reality in an instant, anytime you wish.

5 Allow the story to unfold as long as feels right. With gratitude for what you have discovered, end by taking a deep breath. Open your eyes and stretch your arms and legs. Roll gently to one side and sit up. Make notes or write in your journal about what you have experienced.

Moldavite

Exercise: Blue sky meditation
For this exercise you will need one blue-coloured crystal, such as a piece of polished turquoise or lapis lazuli. As you recall, blue crystals open the throat chakra, encouraging clarity and self-awareness.

1 Sit comfortably on a cushion or a chair with your feet flat on the floor. Hold the turquoise or lapis lazuli crystal to your throat for a few moments. Imagine that you are inhaling the bright blue energy of the crystal, relaxing your throat and enhancing your ability to communicate truthfully with yourself. Then relax and hold the crystal gently in your lap.

2 Bring to awareness whatever thoughts or emotions are passing through your mind at this moment. Do not follow these thoughts or feelings. Simply observe them. Accept whatever arises in your mind.

3 Allow the thought to arise that your mind is like a crystalline blue sky – perhaps the colour of the crystal you are holding. All the thoughts and feelings that pass through your mind are like clouds that move across the sky, coming into view and then passing away. Remind yourself that these passing clouds are not your mind. Your mind is like the sky – vast, clear, empty and filled with light.

4 Focus on the clear blue sky of mind beyond all thoughts and feelings for 10–20 minutes, or until you feel relaxed, aware and at peace.

CRYSTAL MEDITATION

Many people misunderstand the goal of meditation. Meditation is not a passive activity, and although relaxing your body and calming your mind are among its benefits, they are not its central purpose. The aim of meditation is focused awareness – a state of being more present to yourself.

INTERNAL COMMUNICATION

One useful way to think about meditation is as a form of clear internal communication. As you quiet your body and mind and look inside yourself, you become aware that your perceptions, emotions, thoughts and beliefs, including beliefs about yourself such as 'I have a bad temper' or 'I can't manage money', are not permanent and unchanging. Instead, they come and go, like clouds passing across the sky. Crystals can also help this process.

SPIRITUAL CONNECTION

Meditation is also an opportunity to connect with the spiritual realm. Crystals with a high vibration, such as selenite, angelite and celestite, stimulate the higher chakras, lifting you to an awareness of universal consciousness – the realm in which you are simultaneously uniquely yourself and yet one with everything that is.

Connecting with this level of being regularly has the power to transform your life. You realize that you are much more than your physical body and your mind. Like a crystal, you are essentially light energy that has been slowed down or frozen into physical form. Meditation gives your inner light a chance to shine.

Surround yourself with candles and incense to intensify your meditative experience.

DREAM CRYSTALS

Like meditation, dreams allow you to travel beneath the busy surface of consciousness to the depths where currents of insight and understanding flow. Grounding stones such as red jasper and bloodstone stimulate dreaming. Crystals with a higher vibration, such as amethyst, celestite, danburite and moonstone, can help you recall and decode dream messages.

Where do you go in your dreams? Use dream crystals to gain insight from your night-time voyages.

Red jasper

Exercise: Crystal dreaming

For this exercise you will need one piece of red jasper or bloodstone and one piece of amethyst, celestite, danburite or moonstone.

1 Before you go to sleep, place the bloodstone or red jasper under your pillow. Place a notebook and pen near your bed. Allow your last thought before falling asleep to be your intention to dream vividly and to remember your dreams.

2 When you awake, lie still and bring your dreams to mind. Write notes about everything you remember.

3 Later, set aside some time to decode your dreams. Seat yourself comfortably. Place your notebook in your lap and hold the amethyst, celestite, danburite or moonstone crystal in your hands. Close your eyes and breathe in the energy of the crystal until you feel centred and relaxed.

4 Begin by making associations. Assume that every person, place, colour, sound, situation and event in your dream is trying to tell you something. Write down every association you can for each image. An association is any feeling, word, memory or idea that pops up in response to an image.

5 Next, make personal connections. Look over your list of associations and decide which associations 'click' – that is, which spontaneously bring up energy or strong feeling. For each, ask yourself: What part of me is that? What do I have in common with that? Where have I seen that in my life? Make notes about what you discover.

6 Finally, find the message. Use your intuition to draw the associations and connections together into a unified picture. Ask yourself: What message is this dream trying to communicate? What changes is it advising me to make? Don't expect the message to be clear immediately. You'll know you are on the right track when an interpretation gives you a surge of energy.

Clear quartz

Description Long, pointed crystals, clear, glassy, milky or striated. Easily obtained as natural points, clusters or tumbled stones.

Chakra Crown.

History The word 'crystal' comes from krystallos, meaning 'clear ice' in ancient Greek.

Healing attributes Known as the 'master healer', clear quartz can be used to clear blockages, stimulate the immune system, aid concentration and enhance memory.

Moonstone

Description Translucent white, cream or yellow-grey, with an iridescent shimmer. Readily available as natural and tumbled stones.

Chakra Brow and sacral.

History This feminine stone was sacred to ancient moon goddesses such as Aphrodite and Selene.

Healing attributes Moonstone aids a woman's reproductive health and balances hormones. It also eases mood swings and stress, and enhances intuition.

Amethyst

Description Transparent, semi-transparent or translucent crystals ranging from pale lilac and lavender to deep purple. Widely available as a geode, cluster or single point.

Chakra Crown and brow.

History In Tibet, amethyst was sacred to the Buddha and was used to make prayer beads.

Healing attributes A natural tranquillizer, amethyst relieves physical, emotional and psychological stress. Use it to help dispel anger, fear and anxiety and to alleviate sadness.

Aqua aura

Description Clear quartz crystals bonded with gold vapour produce an intense electric or sky-blue colour.

Chakra Crown, brow and throat.

History Although this artificially produced form of quartz is of recent origin, it combines the healing power of quartz with gold, symbol of immortality, health and prosperity.

Healing attributes A protective stone, aqua aura activates the upper chakras and helps safeguard you from pollution and from negative people and situations.

Blue lace agate

Description Pale blue, banded with white or darker blue lines or lacy threads.

Chakra Throat

History Early civilizations in Egypt, Greece and prehistoric Europe created eye bead amulets for protection from evil.

Healing attributes The soft energy of this peaceful stone cools and calms the emotions. It is particularly effective for throat-related ailments. Hold it to your throat to help you speak your truth in public situations.

Sodalite

Description Deep blue or indigo, often with white flecks. Easily obtained as raw or tumbled stones.

Chakra Brow and throat

History Vast deposits of sodalite were discovered in Ontario, Canada, in 1891.

Healing attributes An excellent stone for the mind, sodalite clears mental confusion and supports rational thinking and objectivity. Use its gentle calming and cooling energy to help lower blood pressure and to treat sinus problems.

Blue chalcedony

Description Translucent or semi-translucent in varying shades of soft blue. Available in raw form or as a geode or tumbled stone.

Chakra Throat.

History The name probably comes from Chalcedon, an ancient port city on the Sea of Marmara in Turkey.

Healing attributes A stone of creativity, blue chalcedony stimulates new ideas and helps you to communicate them.

Green fluorite

Description Transparent or semi-transparent cube-shaped or octahedral crystals, sometimes fused into pairs. Some types glow or become 'fluorescent' under ultraviolet light.

Chakra Heart.

History The name is from the Latin fluo, which means 'to flow', because fluorite melts easily.

Healing attributes This stone relieves emotional trauma, heartburn, indigestion, stomach cramps and stress-related ailments. Place it on your computer to absorb negative energy.

Danburite

Description Pink, lilac or clear transparent crystals with striations. Readily available as tumbled stones.

Chakra Crown, brow and heart.

History First discovered in Danbury, Connecticut, USA, this gem has since been found and mined in Japan, Mexico, Burma and Madagascar.

Healing attributes This spiritual stone is a powerful all-body healer that supports the liver and gallbladder and aids detoxification. It also enhances healthy self-esteem.

Citrine

Description Yellow to yellowish-brown quartz. Natural citrine is relatively rare.

Chakra Solar plexus.

History Sacred to the Roman messenger god Mercury, citrine shines the clear light of the morning sun on communication, money and business transactions.

Healing attributes This beneficial stone is warming, uplifting and energizing. It is excellent for the liver, spleen, gallbladder and digestive system.

Carnelian

Description A small smooth translucent pebble, which ranges in colour from clear orange-red to dark orange-brown.

Chakra Sacral and root.

History In Egypt, a carnelian amulet called a tjet, sacred to the goddess Isis, was used to protect the dead on their journey to the afterlife.

Healing attributes This grounding and stabilizing stone increases your metabolism, restores vitality and improves the flow of energy through the body.

Smoky quartz

Description Long, pointed crystals or tumbled stones, from smoky brown to dark grey in colour.

Chakra Root.

History In the United Kingdom, Queen Elizabeth I's court astrologer's crystal ball was smoky quartz. Smoky quartz is also the national gem of Scotland.

Healing attributes This powerful grounding and anchoring stone reduces anxiety and other negative emotions and balances and restores the body's energy.

DIRECTORY OF CRYSTALS FOR EMOTIONS

Apophyllite

Description Clear white cubic or pyramidal crystals, which may have a green, yellow or pink tint.

Chakra Crown.

History Discovered at the start of the 19th century, this crystal's name derives from the Greek word *Apophylliso*, meaning 'it flakes off', a reference to its tendency to flake apart when heated.

Healing attributes The high water content makes this stone an energy conductor. It aids mental clarity and memory.

Lepidolite

Description Layered transparent or translucent, shiny crystals ranging in colour from purple to pink.

Chakra Crown and brow.

History Discovered in the 18th century, the stone has a violet colour which comes from lithium, a mood stabilizer.

Healing attributes Lepidolite clears electromagnetic pollution generated by computers, absorbs stress and helps escape from behavioural patterns, including addictions. This stone also facilitates positive life changes.

Lapis lazuli

Description Deep blue, opaque crystals, often flecked with gold. Readily available in raw or tumbled form, but may be expensive.

Chakra Brow and throat.

History Prized as a gemstone since 5000 BCE, lapis lazuli was sacred to the gods and pharaohs of ancient egypt.

Healing attributes Because of its resemblance to the starry night sky, lapis is considered to be a stone of serenity and peace. It encourages clarity and self-awareness.

Aquamarine

Description Clear, sometimes watery-looking crystal, ranging in colour from light blue to blue-green.

Chakra Throat.

History Latin for 'water of the sea', aquamarine is called the sailor's stone because sailors used it as an amulet to protect themselves from storms and seasickness.

Healing attributes This calming stone brings courage and relieves fears and phobias, especially those connected to travel. It also clears blockages to self-expression.

Rose quartz

Description Translucent pink stone, easily obtained in natural and polished form, often carved into spheres, wands and hearts.

Chakra Heart.

History In myth, this stone is made from the mingled blood of Adonis and Aphrodite – a symbol of love since Roman times.

Healing properties The most important crystal for the heart chakra, calm and peaceful rose quartz opens the heart.

Kunzite

Description Semi-transparent flat or striated crystals, pink to lilac in colour.

Chakra Heart.

History Discovered in California in 1903, this beautiful gem-quality stone was named in honour of New York jeweller and gemstone specialist Dr George Frederic Kunz.

Healing properties A peaceful, loving stone with particular affinity to women, kunzite helps dissolve negativity and heal emotional instability. It also builds confidence.

Amber

Description Organic gemstone, actually the fossilized resin of trees that grew 30 million years ago. translucent yellow or golden orange, sometimes containing fossilized insects or plants. Easily obtained.

Chakra Solar plexus.

History Used throughout history as a protective amulet.

Healing properties A powerful cleanser and healer, this crystal absorbs depression, anxiety and other kinds of emotional distress as well as promoting optimism.

Tiger's eye

Description Yellow crystal with a silky lustre and golden-brown or honey-coloured bands.

Chakra Solar plexus.

History So named because it resembles the eye of a tiger, this attractive stone also imparts a tiger's fearlessness.

Healing properties As a grounding stone, Tiger's eye combines stable earth energy with the energetic power of the sun. it promotes integrity, the proper use of power and finishing what you start. It also balances the emotions.

Labradorite

Description Grey to black stones with iridescent blue or gold flashes.

Chakra Solar plexus.

History The name comes from the Labrador peninsula of Canada, where the stone was discovered.

Healing properties A powerful protector, labradorite deflects negative thoughts and unwanted energy and banishes insecurity and fear. It calms an overactive mind, dispels illusions and balances rational thinking with intuition.

Aragonite

Description In its natural form, this orange to brown crystal often grows as twin crystals or as branching tree or coral-like clusters. Easily obtained.

Chakra Sacral.

History Discovered in Aragon, Spain, it is also found in hot springs, volcanic rocks and caves.

Healing properties A powerful earth healer, this stone keeps you centred and grounded and teaches you to think before you act. It combats anger and bad temper.

Orange calcite

Description Translucent, waxy orange to peach-coloured crystals, often banded with darker orange.

Chakra Sacral.

History One of the most common minerals on earth, calcite is the primary component of cave formations such as stalactites, stalagmites and veils.

Healing properties Excellent for stimulating sexual energies, orange calcite also promotes creativity. It relieves depression and combats fear and phobias.

Bloodstone

Description Also known as heliotrope, this handsome stone is dark green flecked with red or orange. readily available in tumbled form.

Chakra Root and sacral.

History According to Christian myth, when Christ was crucified, his blood fell on a green stone at his feet, which became known as bloodstone.

Healing properties An excellent grounding and protective stone, bloodstone imparts courage.

Selenite

Description White, transparent or semi-transparent. The form called satin spar has fine white bands.

Chakra Crown.

History Named for the moon goddess Selene, selenite symbolizes both change and predictability.

Healing attributes Selenite enhances meditation and psychic communication, including telepathy and clairvoyance, and promotes dream recall. Selenite pillars can be used for crystal gazing.

Moldavite

Description Transparent, deep green, often blackish until held up to light. Rare but readily available. Expensive.

Chakra Crown and brow.

History The properties of this spiritual stone relate to its extraterrestrial origin. It has been used as a good luck and fertility talisman since prehistoric times.

Healing attributes Moldavite's high vibration opens and aligns the chakras and helps clear blockages in the energy pathways. Sometimes called the 'Grail stone'.

Celestite

Description semi-transparent, pale or sky blue with white. sometimes looks like ice crystals.

Chakra Crown, brow and throat.

History The name 'celestite' means 'of the sky'. It was first found in Italy in the 18th century.

Healing attributes Celestite is a wonderful meditation stone. It supports enhanced states of awareness and encourages a feeling of peace and unity. This crystal also enhances personal creative and artistic expression.

Angelite

Description opaque pale blue to blue-violet, with white and sometimes red specks. veins often look like wings.

Chakra Crown, brow and throat.

History Formed from celestite that has been compressed for millions of years, angelite is considered to be the wiser stone of the two.

Healing attributes Called a 'stone of awareness', angelite enhances perception, understanding and telepathic communication between minds and with spiritual beings.

Azurite with Malachite

Description A bright marbled blue and green stone, often with large green flecks and deep azure blue patches.

Chakra Brow.

History For thousands of years this attractive combination stone has been used to make jewellery and ornamental objects.

Healing attributes Like all combination stones, this crystal is more powerful than azurite or malachite alone. It opens the brow chakra to strengthen your ability to visualize and enhances spiritual vision.

Turquoise

Description An opaque light blue and blue green stone, often with darker veins. Easily obtained.

Chakra Throat.

History This stone's history dates back to ancient Egypt, where it was sacred to the goddess Hathor.

Healing attributes This protective and stabilizing stone enhances intuition and communication. It is traditionally believed to unite earth and sky, to harmonize masculine and feminine energies and to balance and align the chakras.

Tourmaline

Description Shiny, opaque or transparent, often with long striations. Many colours, including pink and pink enfolded or banded with green (watermelon tourmaline).

Chakra Heart.

History The last empress of China, Tz'u Hsi, loved pink tourmaline and imported it to China from a mine in California.

Healing attributes This stone aids self-love, relaxation and inner peace. As an aphrodisiac, it helps to harmonize sexuality and spirituality.

Green aventurine

Description Opaque, light to darker green, often speckled with metallic gold or silvery particles. Readily available.

Chakra Heart.

History Green aventurine is often called the 'gambler's stone' because it attracts money and has been found to be lucky in games of chance.

Healing attributes This protective stone heightens perception and stabilizes the mind. It stimulates creativity and optimism and helps you to see alternative possibilities.

Sunstone

Description Transparent or opaque crystal ranging in colour from gentle orange to vivid tangerine with golden iridescent flashes. Easily obtained.

Chakra Solar plexus.

History This ancient gem, said to contain the power of the sun, was believed by the Vikings to be an aid to navigation.

Healing attributes This joyful stone clears the chakras and brings in healing light and energy. it lifts dark moods and depression and attracts good fortune.

Fire opal

Description Usually translucent, milky with dark orange. May have fiery streaks. Easily obtained.

Chakra Sacral.

History Natural healers use fire opal to stimulate the body's energy pathways. It is also said to attract good luck in business.

Healing attributes This protective gem brings joy and enhances personal power and sexual energy. It facilitates life changes and offers support in times of distress.

Red jasper

Description Opaque, solid or patterned, ranging in colour from brick red to brownish red. Easily obtained.

Chakra Root.

History Durable and easily carved, red jasper was popular in antiquity for making seals and decorative inlays.

Healing properties This guardian stone helps you to protect your boundaries and grounds you during visionary journeys and other spiritual work. It helps to cleanse and align the chakras. Placed under your pillow, it promotes dreaming.

Black obsidian

Description Shiny, opaque and glass-like, ranging in colour from black to smoky grey. readily obtained.

Chakra Root.

History Obsidian is formed from molten lava that cooled before it had time to crystallize. For centuries it has been used for crystal gazing and prophecy.

Healing attributes Obsidian works very quickly. Powerful and protective, it encourages deep inner work and helps you to release negative energies.

INDEX